SUPERMAN

WHATEVER HAPPENED TO
THE MAN OF TOMORROW?

WHATEVER HAPPENED TO

written by
Alan MOORE
SUPERMAN

art by
Curt SWAN
Dave GIBBONS
Rick VEITCH
George PÉREZ
Kurt SCHAFFENBERGER
Al WILLIAMSON

colored by
Gene D'ANGELO
Tom ZIUKO
Tatjana WOOD

lettered by
Todd KLEIN
Dave GIBBONS
John COSTANZA

original series cover art by
Curt SWAN
Murphy ANDERSON
Dave GIBBONS
Rick VEITCH

Superman created by **JERRY SIEGEL** and **JOE SHUSTER**
Batman created by **BOB KANE**
Wonder Woman created by **WILLIAM MOULTON MARSTON**
Swamp Thing created by **LEN WEIN**
and **BERNIE WRIGHTSON**

JULIUS SCHWARTZ Editor – Original Series SCOTT NYBAKKEN Editor
ROBBIN BROSTERMAN Design Director – Books ROBBIE BIEDERMAN Publication Design
BOB HARRAS Senior VP – Editor-in-Chief, DC Comics

DIANE NELSON President DAN DIDIO and JIM LEE Co-Publishers GEOFF JOHNS Chief Creative Officer
JOHN ROOD Executive VP – Sales, Marketing & Business Development
AMY GENKINS Senior VP – Business & Legal Affairs NAIRI GARDINER Senior VP – Finance
JEFF BOISON VP – Publishing Planning MARK CHIARELLO VP – Art Direction & Design
JOHN CUNNINGHAM VP – Marketing TERRI CUNNINGHAM VP – Editorial Administration
ALISON GILL Senior VP – Manufacturing & Operations HANK KANALZ Senior VP – Vertigo
& Integrated Publishing JAY KOGAN VP – Business & Legal Affairs, Publishing
JACK MAHAN VP – Business Affairs, Talent NICK NAPOLITANO VP – Manufacturing
Administration SUE POHJA VP – Book Sales COURTNEY SIMMONS Senior VP – Publicity
BOB WAYNE Senior VP – Sales

Cover art by BRIAN BOLLAND,
after CURT SWAN and MURPHY ANDERSON.
Color reconstruction on SUPERMAN 423 and
ACTION COMICS 583 by TOM McCRAW and DIGIKORE.
Color reconstruction on DC COMICS PRESENTS 85 by JAMISON.
Color reconstruction on SUPERMAN ANNUAL 11 by DIGIKORE.

SUPERMAN: WHATEVER HAPPENED
TO THE MAN OF TOMORROW?

DC Comics 1700 Broadway, New York, NY 10019
A Warner Bros. Entertainment Company.
Printed by RR Donnelley, Salem, VA. 11/1/13.
Second printing. ISBN: 978-1-4012-2731-9

SUSTAINABLE
FORESTRY
INITIATIVE
Certified Chain of Custody
At Least 20% Certified Forest Content
www.sfiprogram.org
SFI-01042
APPLIES TO TEXT STOCK ONLY

*This introduction
originally ran in the first
SUPERMAN: WHATEVER HAPPENED
TO THE MAN OF TOMORROW?
collected edition, released in 1997.*

THE TIME HAS COME!

An Introduction by Paul KUPPERBERG

It was in June of 1938 that the first Superman story saw print in ACTION COMICS #1.

It was a little more than forty-eight years later, in ACTION #583, that DC published the "last" Superman story.

Of course, "Whatever Happened to the Man of Tomorrow?" wasn't actually the last Superman story. Obviously, the Man of Steel is still being published, but it was, in its own way, the final story of the Superman that generations of readers had grown up on. The end of an era... at least of that particular era.

A lot of things were changing in comics during the mid-1980s. The way things had been done for the previous fifty or so years had come under the scrutiny of a slew of creators who were finding new ways to do things. Frank Miller's BATMAN: THE DARK KNIGHT RETURNS and Alan Moore and Dave Gibbons's WATCHMEN were essentially redefining the conventions of the super-hero comic, while DC's year-long CRISIS ON INFINITE EARTHS was literally reshaping the DC Universe itself.

And it was CRISIS ON INFINITE EARTHS that was responsible for "Whatever Happened to the Man of Tomorrow?" because in CRISIS, the DC Universe was being streamlined, with decades' worth of multiple-universe continuities and redundant characters being eliminated. No longer was there to be many different Earths set in many different dimensions, each host to many different versions of Batman or Flash or Wonder Woman or Superman. No more would readers have to be conversant with fifty-plus years of characters and continuities in order to read a title. There was to be only one Earth, existing in one universe, featuring (for the most part) only one version of any given character.

As a result of this, it was decided that the post-CRISIS era — in which a character's back story was effectively a blank slate — offered the perfect opportunity to revamp or relaunch a host of DC's top-tier heroes, including Wonder Woman, Flash, Hawkman, the Justice League...

... and Superman.

John Byrne had signed on to write and pencil the relaunched Superman, beginning with THE MAN OF STEEL miniseries that went on sale in July of 1986. This left Superman editor Julius Schwartz with the opportunity to do a grand finale for his stewardship of SUPERMAN and ACTION COMICS. "I started to think, 'What am I going to put in my last two issues?' and in the middle of the night it came to me: I would make believe that *my* last issues of SUPERMAN and ACTION COMICS were *actually* going to be the last issues," Schwartz recalls. "Therefore it was incumbent upon me to clear up, to explain all the things that had been going on in the previous years. For example, did Lois Lane ever find out that Clark Kent was Superman? Did they ever get married? What happened to Jimmy Olsen, to Perry White, to all the villains? I had to clear it up."

With a clear story direction in mind, Julie set out to find a writer to handle the scripting. "I ask this at comic conventions: 'Who would you, sitting in my editorial chair, mid-1985, ask to write that story?'" he chuckles in recollection. The answer was, to Julie, obvious. "He wrote the first one, let him write the 'last' one — Jerry Siegel!" Schwartz happened to be going out to the annual comic book convention in San Diego that year, where one of his fellow guests was to be writer Jerry Siegel, the co-creator (with artist Joe Shuster) of Superman. "Jerry and I spent a lot of time together at the DC booth, and I finally asked him the critical question: Would he be willing to write the 'last' Superman story? Jerry's response was, 'Oh... boy, well, I have to think about that... no, no need to think about it. I would love to write it!' But it turned out there were legal problems that, because of the schedule, we didn't have time to resolve, so Jerry wasn't able to do it after all.

"The next morning, still wondering what to do about it, I happened to be having breakfast with Alan Moore. So I told him about my difficulties. At that point he literally rose out of his chair, put his hands around my neck, and said, 'If you let anybody but me write that story, I'll kill you.' Since I didn't want to be an accessory to my own murder, I agreed."

The fact that Alan Moore was recognized as one of the best writers to work in comics probably had more to do with Julie's decision than fear for his own mortality. Moore had already cemented his reputation as a postmodern master of comics with his work on the British strip *Marvelman* (published in America as *Miracleman*), and his work on DC's SWAMP THING and the aforementioned WATCHMEN was emerging — though both were still in progress — as being among those rare works that would redefine the medium for the future.

..., in a letter to Moore dated September 19, 1985, Julie proclaimed, "The time has come! Meaning — that I've just been informed that the September cover-dated issues of SUPERMAN and ACTION will be my last before John Byrne and Co. take over.

What I'm getting at is: the time has come for you to type up the story your 'mouth' agreed to do — that is, an 'imaginary' Superman that would serve as the 'last' Superman story if the magazines were discontinued — what would happen to Superman, Clark Kent, Lois Lane, Lana Lang, Jimmy Olsen, Perry White, Luthor, Brainiac, Mr. Mxyzptlk, and all the et cetera you can deal with."

The matter of an artist for the 'last' Superman story was never in question. In the preceding thirty years or so, Curt Swan had become, in the minds of generations of readers, the definitive Superman artist, responsible for a staggering number of stories starring the Last Son of Krypton. Certainly if anyone deserved to do the honors on what was sure to become one of the most memorable Superman stories of all time, it was Curt. To this day, more than a decade later, Curt's contribution to the Superman legend stands undiminished even in light of the distinguished artists who have followed in his footsteps. This reprint of his last "official" Superman story is a fitting tribute both to Curt's memory and to his legacy on Superman.

To ink the last Superman stories under his editorial reign, Julie Schwartz called on THE NEW TEEN TITANS co-creator George Pérez for Part One. "George heard I was giving up Superman and had always wanted to ink a Curt Swan story," Julie recalls. Pérez agrees, "It was a dream come true for me to finally get to ink Curt Swan's pencils, especially on his last Superman story, and to work with Alan Moore. Like everyone else, I grew up reading Curt's Superman, so it was thrilling to be working with him on just that level alone. To work with him on this story, which was a bit of history in the making, made it even more special."

Julie chose longtime Superman Family artist Kurt Schaffenberger to ink the concluding chapter because, as he says, "Kurt had been working on Superman material for as long as I can remember, pencilling and/or inking stories with Superman, Lois Lane, Superboy, Supergirl. But it occurred to me that in all those years, Kurt, an excellent inker in his own right, had never inked a Superman story over Swan, so I thought this would be his last ...

... for the covers, Schwartz assigned Murphy Anderson to the inking chores, reasoning that this was the last chance for the classic "Swanderson" (Swan and Anderson) team to strut their stuff on Superman. And, Schwartz points out, if you look closely at the cover of ACTION #583, you'll notice some interesting special appearances. "It shows Superman flying off from the roof of the Daily Planet and everyone waving good-bye. The three people standing in front in the middle are Jenette Kahn, flanked on the left by Curt Swan, and by me (the guy with the glasses) on the right. And in the background are all the super-heroes." And looking closer still, at Superman's face, you'll see tears in the eyes of the Man of Steel. Says Schwartz, "The tears in Superman's eyes are really Curt's tears."

The "last" Superman made quite an impression on most everyone who read it. John Byrne, who was to follow Moore, Swan, Pérez and Schaffenberger saw "Whatever Happened to the Man of Tomorrow?" as a story that no other creators would ever have the chance to do again. "That was the capper, the story that wrapped up the run of the old series, saying good-bye to all the characters the way they had been done and paving the way for what was to come. It's the kind of story that you couldn't normally do, and with a character like Superman, who'll last forever, it's a story the likes of which we'll never see again."

Andrew Helfer, who took over as editor of the Superman line of comics from Julie Schwartz agrees. "It was a unique moment in the history of Superman. In that one moment, we were closing the book on Superman. And in that moment, it really was the last Superman story. It was not an imaginary story. You could utilize all the 'real' things that had preceded it and really create a definitive conclusion for the story of Superman. That only existed as a real story for a moment because right afterwards, the first issue of THE MAN OF STEEL basically defined *all* of the previous Superman stories as imaginary stories. Of course that doesn't mean they were any less valid or any less enjoyable, but they were no longer in continuity, so Alan's story just wonderfully wrapped up the continuity in the way that he seemed best equipped to do.

"Alan, as a master of putting all the little pieces together into a coherent finality, had the ultimate opportunity to take all those hundreds of elements that he had grown up with and wrap them all up in this precious little bundle. It was a ...

As is his wont, Schwartz comes up with the last words on this topic. "In Part One," he says, "in the legend that precedes the story, Alan Moore wrote the truest thing ever said about comics: 'This is an imaginary story. Aren't they all?'"

But the question of imaginary is in the eye of the beholder, and to those reading comics in 1986 when "Whatever Happened to the Man of Tomorrow?" was originally published, this was indeed the "last" Superman story.

Fortunately, for those reading *beyond* 1986, there was a new era waiting beyond it, and, as it turned out, the "last" Superman story merely paved the way for all the great stories that followed.

Paul Kupperberg is a former editor at DC Comics and former executive editor of Weekly World News, *as well as a writer of hundreds of comic books, novels, short stories and miscellany. He is the creator of ARION, LORD OF ATLANTIS, CHECKMATE!, and TAKION. His latest book is* Jewjitsu: The Hebrew Hands of Fury, *published by Citadel Press.*

This is an IMAGINARY STORY (Which may never happen, but then again may) about a perfect man who came from the sky and did only good. It tells of his twilight, when the great battles were over and the great miracles long since performed; of how his enemies conspired against him and of that final war in the snowblind wastes beneath the Northern Lights; of the women he loved and of the choice he made between them; of how he broke his most sacred oath, and how finally all the things he had were taken from him save for one. It ends with a wink. It begins in a quiet midwestern town, one summer afternoon in the quiet midwestern future. Away in the big city, people still sometimes glance up hopefully from the sidewalks, glimpsing a distant speck in the sky... but no: it's only a bird, only a plane. Superman died ten years ago. This is an IMAGINARY STORY...

Aren't they all?

"WHATEVER HAPPENED TO THE MAN OF TOMORROW?"

ALAN MOORE: WRITER

CURT SWAN & GEORGE PÉREZ ARTISTS

TODD KLEIN: LETTERER   **GENE D'ANGELO:** COLORIST

JULIUS SCHWARTZ: EDITOR

IN MEMORIAM

THERE...I THINK THAT SHOULD BE OKAY.

I...I FEEL KINDA *NERVOUS* INTERVIEWING YOU, MRS. ELLIOT. YOU'RE SORT OF A *LEGEND* AROUND THE DAILY PLANET. I'M PROBABLY DOING THIS ALL *WRONG*...

YOU'RE DOING *FINE*... AND IT'S *LOIS.*

LOIS. RIGHT.

UH, WELL, I SUPPOSE I SHOULD START BY ASKING ABOUT THE YEARS LEADING UP TO SUPERMAN'S *DISAPPEARANCE* AND PRESUMED *DEATH.*

WERE THOSE *HAPPY* TIMES?

HAPPY? I DON'T KNOW...THEY WERE A *MIXTURE* OF THINGS, LIKE *MOST* TIMES...

...BUT AT LEAST THEY WERE *QUIET.*

LUTHOR SEEMED TO BE LYING LOW, AND TWO YEARS EARLIER *BRAINIAC'S* LAST ORGANIC METAL BODY HAD BEEN POUNDED INTO A STATE BEYOND *REPAIR.*

AS I RECALL, SUPERMAN LATER RECOVERED EVERY FRAGMENT EXCEPT THE CREATURE'S *HEAD.*

THE PARASITE AND *TERRA-MAN* HAD *DESTROYED* EACH OTHER IN A LETHAL CLASH OF *EGOS*, AND IT SEEMED LIKE THERE WAS NOBODY LEFT TO *FIGHT.*

MOSTLY, SUPERMAN WORKED IN SPACE, DOING *RESEARCH* FOR THE GOVERNMENT.

IT WAS WHILE HE WAS STILL OUT IN SPACE RETURNING FROM SUCH A MISSION THAT WE GOT OUR *FIRST TASTE* OF THE *CARNAGE* THAT WAS TO *FOLLOW...*

GREAT SCOTT.

WHAT'S HAPPENED *HERE?*

SUPERMAN! THANK HEAVENS YOU'RE *BACK!*

YEAH! I TRIED USING MY *SIGNAL-WATCH* EARLIER, BUT I GUESS YOU WERE OUT OF *RANGE...*

BUT THIS *DESTRUCTION...* WHAT *CAUSED* IT? WAS IT A *BOMB,* OR...

WORSE THAN A BOMB. SUPERMAN, IT WAS *BIZARRO!*

BIZARRO DID THIS!

BIZARRO?

HE WAS COMPLETELY *BERSERK,* SMASHING THINGS, *HURTING* PEOPLE, PUSHING OVER *BUILDINGS...* IT WAS *HORRIBLE.* HE KEPT *LAUGHING...*

ABOUT TWENTY *MINUTES* AGO HE RETREATED INTO THAT *DEPARTMENT STORE* AND HASN'T COME OUT *SINCE.*

OKAY. I'M HERE NOW. I'LL HANDLE IT.

BIZARRO.

INCREDIBLE.

BIZARRO?

COME ON OUT AND *SHOW* YOURSELF! I WANT AN *EXPLANATION* FOR THIS!

HA! THAT *EASY!* IT AM PART OF GENIUS BIZARRO *SELF-IMPROVEMENT PLAN!*

BIZARRO--?

SEE, ME SUDDENLY *REALIZE* THAT ME AM NOT *PERFECT* IMPERFECT DUPLICATE! MAYBE ME NOT *TRYING* HARD ENOUGH.

KRUTTUNCH!

EXAMPLE: WHEN YOUR PLANET KRYPTON BLOW UP BY *ACCIDENT,* YOU AM COMING TO EARTH AS *BABY...*

...SO *ME* DECIDE TO BLOW UP WHOLE *BIZARRO WORLD* ON *PURPOSE* AND COME TO EARTH AS *ADULT!*

THE *BIZARRO WORLD?* BLOWN *UP?!*

TH-THAT *RIGHT!* HA HA! PRETTY *IMPERFECT,* HUH?

½ OFF

"YES, I'M TALKING ABOUT THE *UNMASKING*."

DELIVERY FOR MR. *KENT*...

UH, *I'M* CLARK KENT. WHAT *IS* IT?

TWO *PARCELS*, DELIVERED OUTSIDE JUST NOW. THE *BIG* ONE'S REAL *HEAVY*.

CLARK, WE'RE ON THE *AIR* IN THREE MINUTES!

OH, THIS WON'T TAKE A SECOND, LANA. I'LL JUST OPEN THE *LITTLE* ONE, AND...

HMM. THAT'S ODD.

WHAT *IS* IT?

IT'S A LOT OF LITTLE *SUPERMAN ACTION FIGURES*...

OH! I'VE SEEN THOSE *AROUND!* THEY'RE *GREAT!*

HAVE YOU SEEN HOW THEY *WORK?* YOU JUST PRESS THEIR *LEGS* TOGETHER LIKE THIS, AND...

AAAAAA!

WHOOMF

SSIIZZZZIIK

OH.

CLARK...IT WAS *YOU!*

ALL THESE YEARS...IT WAS YOU ALL THE *TIME!*

HA HA! THAT'S *RIGHT*, MISS LANG...

...IT WAS HIM ALL THE *TIME!* HE JUST COMBED HIS *HAIR* AND STUCK ON A PAIR OF *GLASSES!* HA HA HA! WHAT A *GREAT GAG!*

OH, COME *ON!* WE'VE *TOYED* WITH HIM *ENOUGH!*

CLARK... SUPERMAN... THOSE *VOICES...*

YES. I *RECOGNIZE* THEM! THE *TOYMAN* AND THE *PRANKSTER!*

OKAY... HOW DID YOU KNOW THAT I WAS *CLARK KENT?*

HAH! WHAT A *MORON!* WHAT AN *IMBECILE!* WHY DON'T YOU LOOK IN THE *BIG* BOX AND FIND *OUT?*

...AND NO FAIR *PEEKING!* IT'S *LEAD-LINED!*

EVERYBODY STAND *BACK!* IF IT'S A *BOMB*, I'LL CONTAIN THE EXPLOSION.

ALL RIGHT... I'M OPENING IT NOW...

SPRONNNNGGG

NO.... **NO!**

OH, *GOD*...IT'S *PETE*, ISN'T IT? IT'S *PETE ROSS*, AND, AND HE'S *DEAD*...

RI-I-IGHT! BUT NOT BEFORE WE DRAGGED YOUR *SECRET IDENTITY* OUT OF HIM WITH A LITTLE *BOFFO BRAINWASHING!*

WE'D PLANNED TO WORK THROUGH YOUR *FRIENDS*, STARTING WITH THE FURTHEST *AWAY*, BUT WE HIT *PAYDIRT* FIRST *TIME!*

PRANKSTER... TOYMAN...LET ME ASK YOU ONE *QUESTION:*

DO YOU KNOW WHAT *RADIO WAVES* LOOK LIKE?

HUH? NO, WHY?

BECAUSE *I DO!*

YAAAGH!

"THEY GAVE IN ALMOST *IMMEDIATELY*, BUT DIDN'T SEEM ABLE TO TELL HIM *WHY* THEY'D SUDDENLY DECIDED TO START MURDERING HIS *FRIENDS*.

"WHEN HE *ASKED*, THEY JUST LOOKED *DAZED* AND *CONFUSED*.

"...AND, OF COURSE, PUTTING THEM BEHIND BARS DIDN'T MEND THE SENSELESS *DAMAGE* THEY'D CAUSED. PETE ROSS WAS STILL DEAD...

"...AND SO WAS *CLARK KENT*. ONCE PUBLICLY *REVEALED*, HIS SECRET IDENTITY WAS *USELESS*, SO HE *DROPPED* IT."

PLANET
CLARK KENT EXPOSED AS SUPERMAN

"I REMEMBER, AFTER PETE'S *FUNERAL*, HE *TALKED* TO US ALL. ABOUT HIS *FEARS*, HIS *WORRIES*..."

I HAVE *BAD FEELINGS* ABOUT THIS. BIZARRO, THE PRANKSTER, THE TOYMAN... THEY WERE ALL JUST *NUISANCES* BEFORE.

WHAT TURNED THEM INTO *KILLERS*?

ALL THESE *YEARS*, MY GREATEST *NIGHTMARE* HAS BEEN THAT SOMEONE WOULD STRIKE AT ME THROUGH MY *FRIENDS*. NOW IT'S COMING *TRUE*.

LISTEN, BIZARRO'S *DEAD*, THE OTHERS ARE BEHIND *BARS*. WHAT'S TO *WORRY* ABOUT?

I...I DON'T *KNOW*. IT ISN'T *RATIONAL*--IT'S JUST...WELL, IF THE *NUISANCES* FROM MY PAST ARE COMING BACK AS *KILLERS*...

...WHAT HAPPENS WHEN THE *KILLERS* COME BACK?

HE DIDN'T *HAVE* TO MENTION ANY *NAMES*. WE *ALL* KNEW WHO HE WAS TALKING ABOUT. THE *BIG GUNS*: LUTHOR, BRAINIAC... WHAT IF *THEY* CAME BACK MORE VICIOUS THAN EVER?

UH, I THOUGHT BRAINIAC HAD BEEN *DESTROYED*?

"SO DID *WE*...

DEET...
DEET...
DEET...

"...BUT AS WE FOUND OUT *LATER, OTHER* PEOPLE HADN'T GIVEN UP HOPE SO *EASILY.*"

AHA!

DEET...DEET...
DEETDEET
DEET DEET
DEETDEET
DEETDEET

I *KNEW* IT! I *KNEW* YOU HAD TO BE UP HERE *SOMEPLACE.*

HA! I FEEL SOMETHING...JUST A *MOMENT*... UNGHH...

DEEDEET
DEEDEET
DEEDEET

THERE YOU ARE!

TO BE *FRANK*, I'VE SEEN YOU LOOKING *BETTER.*

NOT THAT I'M *COMPLAINING.* I'VE *ALWAYS* WANTED TO OPEN YOU UP AND STUDY THAT *ALIEN TECHNOLOGY.*

NOW THAT YOU'RE *DEAD*, I'M SAVED THE EMBARRASSMENT OF *ASKING.* AND BESIDES...

...I THINK YOU'D HAVE *WANTED* IT THIS WAY.

22

BY HUMAN STANDARDS, YOUR BRAIN IS SUPERB, ITS STORED DATA MASSIVELY USEFUL.

THE KRYPTONIAN HAS INTERRUPTED MY PROGRAMS AND CAUSED ME INDIGNITY. I SHALL TOLERATE HIM NO LONGER.

NOW: RAISE MY FACEPLATE TO YOUR HEAD.

THERE.

MY SHIP WAS DESTROYED BY THE SUPERMAN. OUR FIRST PRIORITY IS TO CONSTRUCT A REPLACEMENT. THE MATERIALS WILL ONLY BE FOUND IN POPULATED AREAS.

TAKE ONE STEP FORWARD.

I FEEL YOU RESISTING ME. IT IS USELESS.

I REPEAT MYSELF: TAKE ONE STEP FORWARD.

VERY GOOD.

NOW ANOTHER STEP.

AND ANOTHER.

AND ANOTHER.

AND ANOTHER...

DEET...
DEET...
DEET...

NATURALLY, WE WEREN'T AWARE OF BRAINIAC'S RETURN UNTIL *LATER.* OVER IN *METROPOLIS*, HOWEVER, WE HAD OUR *OWN* PROBLEMS.

I REMEMBER IT WAS JUST A COUPLE OF DAYS AFTER PETE'S *FUNERAL...*

"THE DAY WHEN SUPERMAN LOST A *PLANET*, FOR THE *SECOND* TIME IN HIS LIFE.

"WE WERE WORKING IN THE OFFICE. THE AIR-CONDITIONING WAS ON THE FRITZ AND THE SIDEWALKS OUT-SIDE WERE *HOT*, THRONGING WITH *PEOPLE...*

"ACCORDING TO LATER REPORTS, CERTAIN MEMBERS OF THE CROWD SUDDENLY STOPPED DEAD AND LOOKED *UPWARDS.*

"IT WAS AS IF SOME *UNSEEN* COMMUNICATION HAD PASSED BETWEEN THEM."

HEY! HEY, *HONEY!* YOU LOOK KINDA *HOT* 'N' *BOTHERED.* COULD YOU USE A *DATE?*

C'MON... WHAT'S TO *LOSE?*

FOR TWENTY BUCKS I COULD BREAK YOUR *HEART.*

I DOUBT IT.

EEEEEEEEE!

SHOOMF

"BY THE TIME WE HEARD THE SCREAMS FROM THE STREET, THE *NIGHTMARE* WAS ALREADY *UNDER WAY*...

SHOOMF SHOOMF SHOOMF

"THERE MUST HAVE BEEN *HUNDREDS* OF THEM...

"AND THEY ALL WANTED ONE THING: *IN!*"

KRITISSHH

GREAT CAESAR'S GHOST! WHAT'S HAPPENING?

CHIEF, THE *BUILDING* ...IT'S UNDER *ATTACK!*

WE'RE BEING *BOARDED* BY *METALLOS!*

WE'RE *COMING,* FRIENDS OF CLARK KENT! WE'RE COMING TO *KILL* YOU, THE WAY KENT KILLED MY *BROTHER!* PREPARE TO BE *MASSACRED,* FOR WE HAVE NO *PITY!*

WE HAVE NO *HEARTS!*

THERE'S TOO *MANY* OF THEM! JIMMY...USE THE *WATCH!*

UNNGH

I *AM!* YOU JUST CAN'T *HEAR* IT! NOBODY CAN...

ZEE ZEE ZEE ZEE ZEE

"...EXCEPT *HIM.*"

ZEE ZEE

ZEE ZEE ZEE ZEE ZEE ZEE

OUT OF MY *WAY*, KID. IT'S THE *WOMAN* I WANT TO KILL *MOST*, THE ALIEN-LOVING TRAMP...

≋UNGH≋

AAA! LET ME *GO!* LET ME...

...*GO*....

"WHAT HAPPENED NEXT HAD ALL THE *FAMILIARITY* OF A *RECURRING DREAM.* I WAS *FALLING*, AND A *VIOLET COMET* WAS FALLING *ALONGSIDE* ME."

"THE REDS AND BLUES RAN *TOGETHER,* YOU SEE, SO THAT'S HOW HE LOOKED WHEN HE *FLEW...*

"...A *VIOLET COMET.*"

HOLD *ON*, LOIS.

I DON'T KNOW HOW *METALLO* CONVERTED SO MANY HUMANS INTO CREATURES LIKE *HIMSELF*, BUT THERE'S A FAST WAY OF *CONTAINING* THEM.

WH-WHATEVER YOU *SAY*.

WHAT ARE YOU DOING...?

RUB ANY IRON ROD IN THE *SAME DIRECTION* FOR *LONG ENOUGH* AND YOU'LL *ALIGN* THE *MAGNETIC POLES* OF THE *PARTICLES,* TURNING IT INTO A *MAGNET...*

...OR IN *THIS* CASE, A *SUPER*-MAGNET.

RRRRK EENNCH

"HE LIFTED THE MAGNETIZED GLOBE INTO THE SKY ABOVE THE *GALAXY* BUILDING.

"I REMEMBER HOPING HE HADN'T MADE IT STRONG ENOUGH TO LIFT THE *CARS* FROM THE STREET *BELOW*, BUT I NEEDN'T HAVE *WORRIED.*

"HE GOT EVERYTHING JUST RIGHT.

"AS ALWAYS!"

"WHEN HE'D GATHERED UP ALL THE *METALLOS*... ALONG WITH MOST *OTHER* METAL FROM THE *PLANET* OFFICES...HE FLEW THE PARALYZED *CYBORGS* TO THE *ST. THERESA PRISON COMPLEX.*

"I GATHER MOST OF THEM WERE LATER SUCCESSFULLY *RE-HUMANIZED.*

"WHEN HE *RETURNED*, HE LOOKED AS *DEVASTATED* AS THE *PLANET* OFFICES.

"HE INSISTED ON TAKING ALL HIS CLOSEST FRIENDS TO THE *FORTRESS OF SOLITUDE*, WHERE HE COULD *DEFEND* THEM IF THE SITUATION CONTINUED TO *WORSEN.*

"HE FETCHED LANA, AND PERRY WHITE'S WIFE, *ALICE.* ALICE AND PERRY WERE NOT QUITE GETTING *ON*, AND SHE WAS VERY *CONFUSED* AND *SCARED.*

"I GUESS WE WERE *ALL* TENSE. EVERYTHING HAD SUCH AN AIR OF *FINALITY*...

"EVENTUALLY WE WERE ALL AT THE *FORTRESS*. I HADN'T BEEN THERE FOR A WHILE, BUT IT WAS STILL THE *SAME...BIG* AND *REMOTE* AND *LONELY*.

"IT WASN'T CALLED THE *FORTRESS OF SOLITUDE* FOR *NOTHING*.

"SHORTLY, *ANOTHER* OLD FRIEND JOINED US. *KRYPTO* HAD BEEN ROAMING THE STARS FOR *YEARS*, BUT NOW HE'D *RETURNED*.

"*WHY*, UNLESS *HE'D* SENSED WHAT THE *REST* OF US HAD? DESPITE OUR WELCOMING HUGS, HIS *ARRIVAL* STRUCK AN *OMINOUS* NOTE ...

"I THINK WE ALL FELT WE'D GOT OUT OF THE CITY JUST IN *TIME*."

Aashid Sofiak

WHERE *IS* HE? WHY DOESN'T THAT *CAPED COWARD* COME OUT AND *DIE* LIKE A *MAN*?

SUBJECT IDENTIFIED. REFERENCE: KRYPTONITE MAN. WE WERE NOT ALONE IN OUR DECISION TO COME HERE.

SUPERMAN HAS APPARENTLY FLED TO THE ARCTIC CIRCLE. THE KRYPTONITE MAN, WHILE INTELLECTUALLY LIMITED, PROVIDES AN IDEAL ASSASSINATION WEAPON.

THIS REMODELED SHIP, THOUGH INFERIOR TO MY ORIGINAL SENTIENT CRAFT, WILL PROVIDE SPEEDIER TRANSPORT TO THE NORTH THAN WHATEVER VEHICLE HE ARRIVED IN.

I PROPOSE WE TAKE HIM WITH US.

YOU HAVE NO OBJECTIONS?

VERY GOOD.

THEN WE SHALL PROCEED.

"EVEN THOUGH IT WAS DEATHLY *SILENT* IN THE *FORTRESS* AT THE TOP OF THE *WORLD*, IF YOU LISTENED *HARD* YOU COULD ALMOST HEAR THE VULTURES GATHERING.

29

"HE PREPARED A MEAL FOR US AND THEN IT WAS TIME FOR BED. HE SHOWED US ALL TO THE *GUEST QUARTERS* AND LOOKED *SAD* AS HE LED *PERRY* AND *ALICE* TO SEPARATE ROOMS.

"I COULDN'T SLEEP, SO I KNOCKED ON THE DOOR OF *LANA'S* ROOM, WHICH WAS NEXT TO MINE. OVER THE YEARS WE'D BEEN *RIVALS*, UNEASY *FRIENDS*, AND FINALLY *STRANGERS*.

"THAT NIGHT, NONE OF IT MATTERED.

"WE BOTH *LOVED* HIM, WE WERE BOTH SCARED THAT HE WAS GOING TO *DIE*, AND AFTER WE'D PUT THAT INTO *WORDS*, WE BOTH *CRIED* AND *HELD* EACH OTHER TILL WE FELL *ASLEEP*.

"AS FOR *SUPERMAN*...

"...WELL, I GUESS *HE* MUST HAVE FELT *RESTLESS* TOO, BUT IN A DIFFERENT *WAY*. I MEAN, WE *ALL* HAD TROUBLE GETTING TO *SLEEP*...

"...BUT *HE* DIDN'T NEED TO SLEEP AT *ALL*."

I'M GLAD YOU CAME BACK, KRYPTO. YOU'RE A PIECE OF MY *LIFE*, YOU KNOW THAT?

HAFF

I DON'T *KNOW*... I FEEL AS IF *ALL* THE PIECES OF MY LIFE ARE FINALLY COMING *TOGETHER*.

YOU KNOW WHAT I MEAN. ANIMALS GET THOSE FEELINGS TOO, WHEN THEY KNOW...

RRRRAFF! RAA-RAFF!

WHAT? WHAT'S THE MATTER? IS SOMETHING...

30

HELLO, KRYPTO! HELLO, BOY! I HOPE YOU AND *STREAKY* AREN'T STILL *SCRAPPING* ALL THE TIME!

SUPERMAN? COULD I HAVE A WORD?

YES. YES, OF COURSE, BRAINIAC.

SUPERMAN, WE WANTED TO PRESENT YOU WITH *THIS,* ON BEHALF OF...

BRAINIAC, WHAT'S THE *MEANING* OF THIS?

YOU *KNOW* SUPERGIRL IS *DEAD* IN THIS ERA. YOU'RE FROM THE *FUTURE.* IT'S *HISTORY* TO YOU!

I--I'M *SORRY.* SHE *INSISTED* ON COMING. I REALIZE HOW *DISTRESSING* IT MUST BE...

I *DOUBT* IT! YOU TALK *CALMLY* TO US, ALL THE WHILE KNOWING OUR *DEATH DATES* AS *ANCIENT HISTORY.* HOW CAN YOU *DO* IT?

SUPERMAN, YOU ARE BEING *UNFAIR.*

IN *YOUR* PAST, AS *SUPERBOY,* YOU HAVE SEEN SOME OF *OUR* FUTURE. WOULD *YOU* TELL *US* IF YOU KNEW OF SOME *UNAVOIDABLE DOOM* AWAITING US?

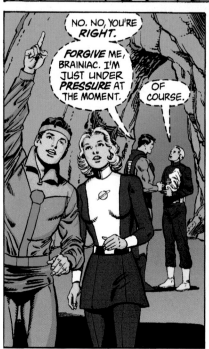

NO. NO, YOU'RE *RIGHT.*

FORGIVE ME, BRAINIAC. I'M JUST UNDER *PRESSURE* AT THE MOMENT.

OF COURSE.

NOW, LET ME GIVE YOU *THIS* ON BEHALF OF THE *LEGION.* IT'S THE REASON WE *CAME* TO THIS PERIOD.

WELL, *THANK* YOU, BUT...

...WHY DID YOU CHOOSE *THIS* PARTICULAR DATE TO *PRESENT* IT TO ME?

W-WELL, BECAUSE OUR *HISTORIES* MARK THIS DATE AS A SPECIAL *TIME* IN YOUR *LIFE.* THEREFORE, WE CAME HERE TO *MEET* WITH YOU AGAIN, AND *SALUTE* YOU... AND...

...AND PAY YOUR *LAST* RESPECTS.

IS *THAT* IT?

COUSIN--?

I JUST *THOUGHT* OF SOMETHING...

AS THE SUPERGIRL OF *THIS* ERA, AM I AWAY VISITING ANOTHER *TIME PERIOD* OR SOMETHING? BECAUSE *I* THOUGHT YOU COULDN'T MATERIALIZE IN AN ERA WHERE YOU ALREADY *EXISTED.*

UH, YES. YES, YOU'RE *RIGHT...*

RIGHT NOW, SUPERGIRL... SUPERGIRL IS IN THE *PAST.*

UH, PERHAPS WE'D BEST RETURN YOU TO OUR *30TH CENTURY,* TO PREVENT ANY *PROBLEMS* SHOULD THIS ERA'S *SUPERGIRL* RETURN, UH, UNEXPECTEDLY.

OH, WELL, I GUESS SO. GIVE ME MY *REGARDS* WHEN I RETURN FROM THE *PAST.*

GOOD-BYE, SUPERMAN. WE... WE *ALWAYS* MISS YOU.

BRAINIAC, CAN WE *GO?* M-MY *EYES* ARE WATERING. MUST BE SOME 20TH-CENTURY *VIRUS...*

"HE NEVER TOLD ME EXACTLY WHAT *HAPPENED* THAT NIGHT BEFORE THE *SIEGE* BEGAN, BUT AS SOON AS I SAW HIM THE NEXT MORNING, I KNEW *SOMETHING* HAD UPSET HIM.

"HE LOOKED *FUNNY.*"

"HE LOOKED AS IF HE'D BEEN *CRYING*."

MORE *COFFEE*, TIM? INTERVIEWS ALWAYS MAKE ME SO *DRY*, WHAT WITH ME DOING ALL THE *TALKING*.

YOU MUST BE *VERY* BORED.

OH, *NO!* NO, IT'S JUST WHAT THE *PLANET'S* MEMORIAL EDITION *NEEDS*.

I'M JUST CHECKING WHERE WE'D GOT TO... SUPERMAN'S OLD *ENEMIES* HAD STARTED RETURNING WITH A *VENGEANCE* AND HE'D TAKEN EVERYONE TO HIS *FORTRESS*, FOR SAFETY.

THAT'S *RIGHT.* ME, LANA, JIMMY, PERRY AND ALICE WHITE... ALL HIS *FRIENDS.* WE WERE ALL...,

SAY, *IZZAT COFFEE* I SMELL BREWIN' THROUGH HERE?

HA HA! BEST DARN NOSE FOR *COFFEE* IN THE WHOLE OF *PITTSDALE.* YOU'LL HAVE TO FIX IT *YOURSELF*, HON. I'M BUSY BEING A *CELEBRITY.*

TIM, THIS IS MY HUSBAND, *JORDAN.*

JORDY, THIS IS *TIM CRANE*, FROM THE *PLANET.*

OH. HI.

UHH.., I HOPE YOU DON'T MIND ME INTERVIEWING YOUR *WIFE* ABOUT, WELL, ABOUT...,

ABOUT HER *EX? NAH!* I CAN *LIVE* WITH IT. HE WEREN'T NOTHIN' *SPECIAL.* US ORDINARY WORKIN' *SLOBS*, SON... *WE'RE* THE *REAL* HEROES.

NOW, JORDY, DON'T YOU GET STARTED IN ON *THAT!* YOU JUST FIX YOUR *COFFEE* THEN GO AND CHECK THAT *JONATHAN'S* STILL ASLEEP.

WHERE HAD I *GOT* TO, TIM?

UH...YOU WERE ALL UP IN THE *ARCTIC*, WITH *SUPERMAN*...

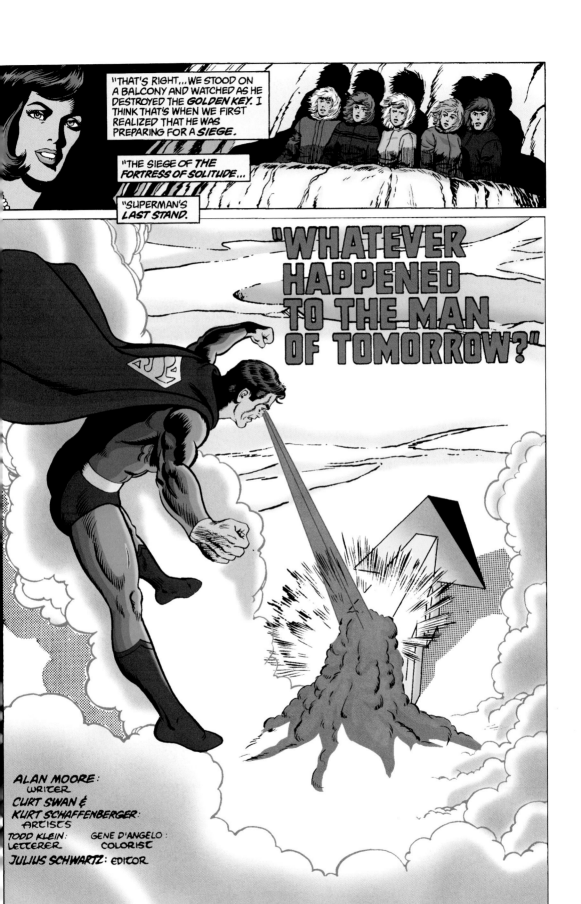

"THAT'S RIGHT...WE STOOD ON A BALCONY AND WATCHED AS HE DESTROYED THE *GOLDEN KEY.* I THINK THAT'S WHEN WE FIRST REALIZED THAT HE WAS PREPARING FOR A *SIEGE.*

"THE SIEGE OF *THE FORTRESS OF SOLITUDE...*

"SUPERMAN'S *LAST STAND.*

"WHATEVER HAPPENED TO THE MAN OF TOMORROW?"

ALAN MOORE: WRITER

CURT SWAN & KURT SCHAFFENBERGER: ARTISTS

TODD KLEIN: LETTERER   GENE D'ANGELO: COLORIST

JULIUS SCHWARTZ: EDITOR

"ALL THAT DAY, IN THE FORTRESS, PERRY AND ALICE KEPT *BICKERING.* EVERYBODY WAS SO *TENSE.*"

"WE WERE *SCARED.* WE KNEW THAT *SOMETHING* WAS BEARING DOWN ON US, BUT WE DIDN'T KNOW *WHAT...*"

"...AND EVEN IF WE *HAD* KNOWN, WE WOULDN'T HAVE FELT ANY *BETTER.*"

ASSESSMENT: THE KRYPTONIAN HAS GONE TO GROUND. I MUST CONSIDER OUR NEXT MOVE.

WHAT'S TO *CONSIDER?* I WANT MY *HANDS* AROUND HIS *THROAT!* I WANT TO WATCH HIM TURN *GREEN* AND *DIE!*

YOU WILL DO AS I COMMAND, KRYPTONITE MAN. WITH LUTHOR'S MIND AT MY DISPOSAL, MY INTELLECT IS SUPREME. I SHALL DEVISE A PLAN COVERING ALL EVENTUALITIES.

A-ALL EVENTUALITIES, BRAINIAC?

EVEN *THAT* ONE?

ALERT. PROBABILITY OF ATTACK: *74.012 PERCENT...*

HOLD YOUR *FIRE,* LUTHOR. WE COME AS *ALLIES* TO *JOIN* YOU IN THE *ASSURED* AND *PREDESTINED* SLAUGHTER OF *SUPERMAN.*

HAVE YOU FORGOTTEN THE *FUTURE,* LUTHOR? DON'T YOU REMEMBER THE *LEGION OF SUPER-VILLAINS?*

MEKT, WAIT...

I--I'M SCANNING LUTHOR'S *MIND*... IT'S BEING *DOMINATED* BY SOMETHING *COLD, EMOTIONLESS*...

ON HIS *HEAD*...IS THAT SOME SORT OF *HELMET*, OR...?

LEX LUTHOR IS NOW MERELY THE VESSEL OF BRAINIAC.

QUERY: WHAT MANNER OF BEINGS ARE YOU?

W-WE ARE *SATURN WOMAN, LIGHTNING LORD,* AND *COSMIC KING,* FROM THE *30TH* CENTURY...

ACCORDING TO *LEGEND,* DURING THESE DAYS, SUPERMAN MET HIS *GREATEST FOE* IN BATTLE AND WAS *NO MORE.*

CERTAIN OF *VICTORY,* WE'VE COME TO *PARTIC-IPATE.*

HIS GREATEST FOE? OF COURSE. I SHRUNK KANDOR. I WAS ALWAYS HIS GREATEST FOE.

QUERY: WHY SHOULD I PERMIT YOU TO SHARE MY VICTORY?

BECAUSE WE'RE FROM THE *FUTURE.* WE *KNOW* THINGS.

FOR *EXAMPLE,* IT'S *SAID* THAT DURING SUPERMAN'S *LAST DAYS,* ALL OF EARTH'S *CHAMPIONS* FLOCKED TO *HELP* HIM...

THAT IS LOGICAL. THIS WORLD'S OTHER SUPER-HUMANS ARE CERTAIN TO INTERFERE.

I SHALL ERECT AN IMPENETRABLE FORCE-SCREEN IMMEDIATELY.

FOR RESISTING MY WILL; FOR DESTROYING MY BODY; FOR THESE AFFRONTS SHALL THE KRYPTONIAN KNOW THE REVENGE OF BRAINIAC...

...AND NONE SHALL HELP HIM.

"WHEN THE FORTRESS' *SENSORS* REGISTERED BRAINIAC'S *FORCE-SCREEN,* WE KNEW IT HAD *BEGUN.*

"THE SCREEN TOOK THE FORM OF A GIANT BUBBLE, MORE THAN TWO MILES ACROSS. NOTHING COULD GET IN. NOTHING COULD GET *OUT.*

"AROUND *NOON*, THE VILLAINS BEGAN FIRING ON THE *FORTRESS* USING WEAPONS FROM BRAINIAC'S *SHIP.*

"SUPERMAN *DESTROYED* MOST OF THE DEVICES FROM *LONG RANGE*, USING *HEAT VISION*, BUT THE *FORCE-SCREEN* GENERATOR WAS TOO WELL *SHIELDED.*

"DURING THE AFTERNOON, HE TOOK *KRYPTO* AND ATTEMPTED A *FRONTAL ASSAULT*, BUT THEY WERE DRIVEN *BACK* BY THE *KRYPTONITE MAN.*

"HIS *POWERS* SEEMED TO HAVE INCREASED *TENFOLD.* THEY COULDN'T EVEN GET *NEAR* HIM.

"WITH *TWILIGHT, OTHER* HEROES BEGAN ARRIVING OUTSIDE THE *BARRIER.* THOSE THAT WERE HIS *FRIENDS...*

"THOSE THAT WERE ALMOST HIS *RIVALS...*

"...THOSE THAT MIGHT HAVE BEEN HIS *LOVERS.* IT DIDN'T MATTER. *NONE* OF THEM COULD *PENETRATE* IT.

"AS NIGHT FELL, IT SEEMED THAT A *STANDOFF* HAD BEEN DECLARED, AND THERE WAS A *LULL* IN THE *BATTLE.* WE *ALL* KNEW IT WOULDN'T LAST LONG.

"WE FIGURED WE HAD AT LEAST UNTIL *MORNING*, SO WE DECIDED TO GET SOME *SLEEP...*

"...BUT SUPERMAN AND PERRY WEREN'T THE *ONLY* ONES WHO COULDN'T SLEEP THAT NIGHT."

LANA? WHAT ARE *YOU* DOING UP HERE?

WELL, IF THAT *FLASK* IN YOUR HAND'S WHAT I *THINK* IT IS, I'M DOING THE SAME THING AS *YOU.* I'M *SICK* OF SITTING AROUND. I WANT TO *HELP* HIM.

THAT'S THE *ELASTIC LAD SERUM,* ISN'T IT?

YES. I *KNEW* HE KEPT A SAMPLE IN HIS *TROPHY ROOM ANNEX,* SO I CAME TO *FIND* IT.

ALL THESE YEARS, THEY'VE CALLED ME *"SUPERMAN'S FRIEND."* I FIGURE HERE'S WHERE I START *PAYING* FOR THE PRIVILEGE.

HOW ABOUT *YOU?*

ELASTIC LAD SERUM

I HAD THE SAME *IDEA.* I REMEMBER YEARS AGO, THERE WERE TIMES WE GAINED *SUPER-POWERS* TEMPORARILY. I REMEMBER THERE WAS THIS *LAKE* THAT *LOIS* AND I BATHED IN ...

"MAGIC" LAKE WATER (PROBABLE UNIDENTIFIED RADIATION SOURCE.)

HEY,...LOOK! HERE'S A CASE OF SOUVENIR *COSTUMES!*

THEN WE'RE IN *LUCK!*

TURN YOUR BACK, *RED,* WHILE I TAKE A QUICK *DIP.*

OH.

OH, THE *FEELING.* I *REMEMBER* NOW... MY *SKIN,* TINGLING AS IT GETS *HARDER....* MY *SENSES* EXPANDING... X-RAY VISION... MICROSCOPIC VISION...

"...SUPER-HEARING..."

YOU SEE, BACK WHEN I WAS *SUPERBOY*, LANA WAS THE ONLY GIRL I *LOVED*.

SHE STILL REPRESENTS *SMALLVILLE* TO ME, THAT PART OF MY *LIFE*, AND *BECAUSE* OF THAT I COULD *NEVER* CAST HER ASIDE.

...BUT SINCE I'VE *GROWN* AND BECOME A *MAN*, THERE'S ONLY EVER BEEN *ONE* WOMAN FOR ME.

LOIS. BEAUTIFUL *LOIS.*

I *LOVE* HER, PERRY. DEAR GOD, I LOVE HER SO *MUCH...*

"...BUT I CAN'T *TELL* HER WITHOUT HURTING *LANA.* I'D *NEVER* HURT LANA, SO I JUST WALK AROUND WITH THIS *SECRET,* THIS *WEIGHT* IN MY *HEART...*

"...AND I'LL CARRY IT WITH ME TO MY *GRAVE...*

"...AND *NEITHER* OF THEM WILL EVER *KNOW.*

THERE. ARE YOU READY YET, LANA?

LANA? IS ANYTHING *WRONG?*

WRONG? NO. NO, WHY SHOULD ANYTHING BE *WRONG?*

I'M *READY* NOW. LET'S GET OUT THERE, WRECK THAT *FORCE-SCREEN,* AND GET HIM *OUT* OF THIS MESS. WE'RE ONLY *SECOND STRINGERS,* JIMMY, BUT *WE'LL* SHOW 'EM...

NOBODY LOVED HIM BETTER THAN *US.*

NOBODY!

HE'S. DEAD.

BUT WHO...?

WHO... ...DO YOU... ...SUPPOSE...?

I...AM BRAINIAC... REDUCER OF KANDOR...AND HIS GREATEST FOE...

MY VICTORY... IS PREORDAINED. DO YOU THINK... THAT I WOULD LET...THE DEATH... OF THIS BODY... STAND IN ITS WAY?

OH MERCIFUL CREATOR...

LUTHOR'S NERVES... HIS MUSCLES... ARE INTACT. I CAN... MANIPULATE THEM...

...AT LEAST,,, FOR LONG ENOUGH...TO ENSURE... SUPERMAN'S DESTRUCTION.

BRAINIAC? SOMETHING'S WRONG. IF OLSEN WRECKED THE GENERATOR, WHY HASN'T THE FORCE-SCREEN COLLAPSED?

"ANALYSIS: YOU ARE CORRECT,,,EARTH'S CHAMPIONS REMAIN OUTSIDE...SOME UNKNOWN FORCE MAINTAINS THE SHIELD,,,

"PERHAPS...PERHAPS IT IS DESTINY. IN ANY EVENTUALITY,,,WE MUST MAKE USE OF IT,,,WHILE THIS FLUKE SITUATION ...ENDURES."

PREPARE...FOR A NUCLEAR STRIKE...

OUR FINAL ASSAULT,,, BEGINS,,,

"...WE HAD OUR *OWN* PROBLEMS."

SUPERMAN... WHAT'S HAPPENING? WHERE ARE LANA AND THE OTHERS?

I...I DON'T KNOW. PERRY AND ALICE AREN'T HURT, BUT I CAN'T SEE LANA OR JIMMY ANYWHERE. MAYBE THEY FLED...

TITANO

LORI LEMARIS

...OR MAYBE THEY'RE DEAD!

AAA!

HA HA HA HA HA! WANT TO BUY YOURSELF SOME TIME, KRYPTONIAN?

WHY NOT THROW ME THE WOMAN, SO I CAN FRY HER THE WAY I FRIED YOUR OTHER GIRLFRIEND?

L-LANA?

YOU HURT LANA?

AAAAA! HE BURNED ME! HE BURNED ME!

HIS MIND... HE ISN'T BLUFFING... HE'S PREPARED TO KILL!

M-MAYBE THIS WASN'T SUCH A GOOD IDEA. FROM OUR LEGENDS, I'D EXPECTED A QUICK VICTORY...BUT THIS IS DANGEROUS!

LET'S GET OUT OF HERE. WE KNOW THAT BRAINIAC WILL WIN... THERE'S NO SENSE GETTING HURT IN THE PROCESS.

"BY THE TIME WE'D FOLLOWED THEM *OUTSIDE*, THEIR *BUBBLE* WAS ALREADY VANISHING BACK TO THE 30TH CENTURY..."

"...AND THERE WAS ONLY ONE FOE LEFT TO *FACE*.

"OR MAYBE *TWO*."

ANALYSIS: STIFFENING...OF LIMBS...DIFFICULTY...IN MOVEMENT. *ASSESSMENT:* ONSET...OF RIGOR MORTIS... IN HOST BODY...IMMINENT.

OH, GOD, *LOOK* AT IT!

BUT...THE VILLAINS FROM THE FUTURE...THEY SAID YOU WOULD MEET...YOUR GREATEST FOE IN BATTLE... AND BE NO MORE. ME. BRAINIAC. YOUR GREATEST FOE...

I AM PREDESTINED... TO DESTROY YOU...

LOIS, GET *BACK!* HE'S *FALLING!*

NO! GET...UP! GET UP...LUTHOR. I...WILL NOT BE BETRAYED...BY YOUR...HUMAN WEAKNESS...

WHERE...IS MY KRYPTONITE MAN...? WHY...IS MY FORCE-SCREEN...STILL STANDING...? I DON'T KNOW...I DON'T CARE...

I...AM COMING FOR YOU... KRYPTONIAN... MY VICTORY...IS INEVITABLE...

SUPERMAN? IT'S CRAWLING *OFF* HIM...

CLINK RINK PLITTINK

IT'S OKAY, LOIS. I... I DON'T THINK HE'S IN ANY CONDITION TO HARM US.

SHRING CHLINK K'INGLE TUNG

"THE DISINTEGRATING COLLECTION OF PLATES AND CIRCUITS CRAWLED A COUPLE OF INCHES, PROPELLED BY SHEER MALICE, THEN STOPPED MOVING.

"BRAINIAC WAS *DEAD*.

"IT WAS ALL OVER...

"WHEN THE SMOKE FINALLY CLEARED, HE WAS JUST *SITTING* THERE, IN THE *AIR*. HE LOOKED *DIFFERENT* SOMEHOW. HE DIDN'T LOOK *FUNNY* ANYMORE."

SO, YOU FINALLY *GUESSED!*

GREETINGS, SUPERMAN. GREETINGS FROM THE *FIFTH DIMENSION.*

YOU WERE *GUIDING* ALL THIS, FROM BEHIND THE *SCENES?* ALL THIS *KILLING* AND *DESTRUCTION?*

MXYZPTLK, IN RAO'S NAME, *WHY?*

DON'T BE *NAIVE*, SUPERMAN. I'M AN *IMMORTAL*, LIKE *EVERYONE* IN THE *FIFTH DIMENSION.*

THE BIG *PROBLEM* WITH BEING *IMMORTAL* IS FILLING YOUR *TIME*. FOR *EXAMPLE*, I SPENT THE *FIRST* TWO THOUSAND YEARS OF MY EXISTENCE DOING ABSOLUTELY *NOTHING.*

I DIDN'T *MOVE*...I DIDN'T EVEN *BREATHE.*

EVENTUALLY, SIMPLE *INERTIA* BECAME *TIRESOME*, SO I SPENT THE *NEXT* TWO THOUSAND YEARS BEING *SAINTLY* AND *BENIGN*, DOING ONLY *GOOD DEEDS.*

WHEN *THAT* NOVELTY BEGAN TO FADE, I DECIDED TO TRY BEING *MISCHIEVOUS.*

NOW, TWO THOUSAND YEARS *LATER*, I'M *BORED* AGAIN. I NEED A *CHANGE*. STARTING WITH YOUR *DEATH*, I SHALL SPEND THE NEXT TWO MILLENNIA BEING *EVIL!*

AFTER *THAT*, WHO *KNOWS?* PERHAPS I'LL TRY BEING *GUILTY* FOR A WHILE.

DID YOU *HONESTLY BELIEVE* A FIFTH-DIMENSIONAL *SORCERER* WOULD RESEMBLE A *FUNNY LITTLE MAN* IN A *DERBY HAT?* WOULD YOU LIKE TO SEE HOW I *REALLY* LOOK?

SUPERMAN...H-HE'S *CHANGING!*

WE'D BETTER GET *INSIDE*...

"I CAN'T DESCRIBE WHAT MXYZPTLK *BECAME*. IT HAD *HEIGHT, LENGTH, BREADTH,* AND A COUPLE OF *OTHER* THINGS."

"AS WE ENTERED THE FORTRESS I GLANCED BACK. IT WAS *FOLLOWING* US. LOOKING AT IT MADE MY *HEAD* HURT."

WHY *STRUGGLE?* YOU *KNOW* THERE'S NO *ESCAPE*. TODAY YOU MEET YOUR *GREATEST FOE*, AND SHALL BE *NO MORE*.

WHY, THE WHOLE *30TH CENTURY* KNOWS IT!

"HE SHOULDN'T HAVE MENTIONED THE *30TH CENTURY!* THAT WAS HIS *MISTAKE*.

"*REMINDED*, I LOOKED AT THE *STATUETTE* IN MY *HANDS*..."

LOIS, HE'S *MAGICAL*. I CAN'T *BEAT* HIM. *RUN!* I'LL HOLD HIM OFF AS LONG AS POSSIBLE...

NO! WAIT! THIS *STATUETTE* ...WHY DID THEY *GIVE IT* TO YOU?

AS A *TRIBUTE*... ALTHOUGH THEY MUST HAVE *KNOWN* HOW MUCH IT WOULD *DISTURB* ME.

EXACTLY! SO MAYBE THEY GAVE YOU IT FOR *ANOTHER* REASON...SOME KIND OF *HINT*, MAYBE?

TAKE ANOTHER *LOOK* AT IT, SUPERMAN!

LOOK AT WHAT IT'S *HOLDING!*

HIS SUPREME HOUR

"HE LOOKED AT THE GOLDEN FIGURINE, AT THE GOLDEN DEVICE IN ITS HANDS. HIS EYES NARROWED, EVER SO SLIGHTLY. HE *KNEW*.

"HE KNEW WHAT HAD TO BE *DONE*."

THIS WAY! IF WE CAN ONLY GET TO THE CHAMBER IN *TIME*!

WHUURP

"THE CHAMBER, WHEN WE REACHED IT, WAS AS *EERIE* AND *UNPLEASANT* AS I REMEMBERED. FROM A SCREEN AT ONE END, PALE MEN WITH MURDEROUS EYES MOUTHED *OBSCENITIES* AT US."

"*TIME* WAS RUNNING *OUT*..."

"...AND THEN, SUDDENLY, IT WAS ALL *GONE*."

AHH, THERE YOU ARE.

TIME TO *DIE*, I THINK.

THAT'S RIGHT, MXYZPTLK.

TIME TO DIE.

"HE TURNED, THE *PHANTOM ZONE PROJECTOR'S* SINGLE CYCLOPS EYE STARING FROM BETWEEN HIS HANDS, FINGER MOVING TOWARDS ITS *BLACK BUTTON*. MXYZPTLK HAD NO MEANS OF *ESCAPE*..."

"...EXCEPT *ONE*!"

KLTPZYXM!

"WITH THE UTTERANCE OF HIS REVERSED NAME, THE CREATURE'S *MAGIC* RETURNED HIM TO THE *FIFTH DIMENSION*..."

"...WHILE AT THE SAME INSTANT THE *RAY* SENT HIM INTO THE *PHANTOM ZONE*."

YEEEAAARRGH

THAT TERRIBLE *SCREAM*. IS HE...?

TORN IN *HALF*, BETWEEN *DIMENSIONS*. HE PANICKED WHEN HE SAW THE *RAY* AND MADE A *FATAL ERROR*. JUST AS I *KNEW* HE WOULD.

I *KILLED* HIM, LOIS! I *INTENDED* TO KILL HIM!

I JUST COULDN'T RISK LETTING ANYTHING THAT *POWERFUL* AND *MALIGNANT* SURVIVE, SO I MADE UP MY *MIND*, AND I *DID* IT.

B-BUT YOU *HAD* TO! YOU HAVEN'T DONE ANYTHING *WRONG*...

I BROKE MY *OATH*. I *KILLED* HIM.

YES, I HAVE.

NOBODY HAS THE RIGHT TO KILL. NOT *MXYZPTLK*, NOT *YOU*, NOT *SUPERMAN*...

ESPECIALLY NOT SUPERMAN!

"HE TURNED AND WALKED AWAY, IN COMPLETE SILENCE. I RAN *AFTER* HIM, CALLING HIS *NAME*.

"HE DIDN'T *REPLY*...

"...AND BY THE TIME I REALIZED WHERE HE WAS *HEADING*, IT WAS *TOO LATE*.

GOLD KRYPTONITE
SAMPLE STORAGE CHAMBER
KEEP OUT!

"AS HE WALKED INTO THE BLINDING GOLDEN LIGHT HE *TURNED*, AND LOOKED BACK OVER HIS *SHOULDER*. HE *SMILED* AT ME...

"I NEVER SAW SUPERMAN AGAIN.

"WITH MXYZPTLK'S *DESTRUCTION*, THE *FORCE-SCREEN* HIS MAGIC HAD BEEN MAINTAINING *VANISHED*, AND THE HEROES *OUTSIDE* WERE FREE TO *ENTER*.

"YOU PROBABLY *READ* ABOUT WHAT THEY *FOUND*...

"THE WRECKAGE IN AND AROUND THE FORTRESS SEEMED TO BE STREWN WITH *BODIES*. THOSE OF HIS MOST BITTER *ENEMIES*...

"...AND THOSE OF HIS MOST *LOYAL FRIENDS*. I REMEMBER THE *BATMAN* DESCRIBING IT AS '*LIKE WALKING AMONGST THE FRAGMENTS OF A LEGEND*.'

"DEATH AND DESTRUCTION WERE EVERYWHERE...

" ...ALMOST.

"*ALMOST* EVERYWHERE.

"THEY FOUND ME OUTSIDE THE LOCKED *GOLD KRYPTONITE CHAMBER*, WEEPING. WHEN *SUPERWOMAN* AND *CAPTAIN MARVEL* RIPPED THE VAULT *OPEN*, IT WAS *EMPTY*.

"HE WAS GONE."

THEY DISCOVERED A *HIDDEN PASSAGEWAY*, LEADING OUT OF THE *FORTRESS*, AND IT WAS FINALLY CONCLUDED THAT HE'D WALKED OUT *POWERLESS* INTO THE SUBZERO WASTES TO *FREEZE*.

THEY NEVER FOUND HIS BODY.

MORE *COFFEE*, TIM?

UH, NO, IT'S GETTING PRETTY *LATE* AND I THINK THE *INTERVIEW'S* ALMOST *THROUGH.*

TELL ME, MRS. ELLIOT, WHAT DO *YOU* THINK OF THE *RUMORS* THAT SUPERMAN IS STILL *ALIVE* SOMEWHERE?

WELL, I'M SURE A LOT OF PEOPLE WOULD *LIKE* TO BELIEVE THAT...

...BUT AS FAR AS I'M CONCERNED, SUPERMAN DIED IN THE *ARCTIC.*

I WAS *THERE.*

OF *COURSE.* I--I'M *SORRY* IF THAT LAST QUESTION WAS *TACTLESS.* YOU JUST HEAR A LOT OF *TALK...*

I GUESS IT'S THE SAME AS WITH *JIM MORRISON* OR *BRUCE LEE,* ALL THOSE OLD *RUMORS...*

HEEEEEERE'S JOHNNY!

WHAT...? *OH!* JONATHAN... YOU'RE *AWAKE!* HAVE YOU GOT A KISS FOR *MOMMY?*

A BAH!

UH, WELL, LISTEN, I OUGHT TO BE GOING. I'LL SEND YOU A COPY OF THE *INTERVIEW* TO CHECK ONCE I'VE *TRANSCRIBED* IT.

WELL, IF YOU GET *TIME.* I KNOW WHAT IT'S *LIKE.* GIVE MY LOVE TO THE *PLANET.*

I WILL. THANKS FOR *EVERYTHING,* MRS. ELLIOT. YOU *TOO,* MR. ELLIOT. I'LL BE IN *TOUCH.*

'BYE, FELLA. NICE *MEETIN'* YA.

DAH!

58

WELL, HE'S *GONE*. I GUESS THE *MEDIA* WON'T BE *BOTHERING* US FOR ANOTHER TEN YEARS NOW.

LET'S *HOPE* SO.

DOWN YOU *GO*, JONATHAN. YOU *PLAY* FOR A WHILE.

SO, HOW WAS *WORK* TODAY?

GREAT. OLD *DAN HODGE* BROUGHT IN SOME *SNAPSHOTS* OF HIS *GRAND-CHILDREN,* AND WE'RE WORKING ON THIS OLD '48 BUICK AT THE MOMENT, TRYING TO GET HER *WORKING.*

SHE'S *BEAUTIFUL.*

YOU REALLY *LOVE* IT, DON'T YOU? JUST GOING TO *WORK* EVERY DAY, TAKING OUT THE *GARBAGE,* CHANGING JONATHAN'S *DIAPERS*... ALL THIS *NORMAL* STUFF.

YUP. CAN'T *BEAT* IT... ALTHOUGH MAYBE I COULD LIVE WITHOUT THE *DIAPERS.*

HMMM. YOU KNOW, YOU WERE PRETTY HARD ON *SUPERMAN* EARLIER.

SUPERMAN? HE WAS *OVERRATED,* AND TOO *WRAPPED UP* IN HIMSELF. HE THOUGHT THE WORLD COULDN'T GET ALONG *WITH-OUT* HIM.

WHAT'S FOR *DINNER?*

PIZZA. AFTER *THAT,* IF *JONATHAN'S* QUIET, I THOUGHT MAYBE *BED* WITH A BOTTLE OF *WINE,* AND AFTER *THAT,* I FIGURE WE JUST LIVE HAPPILY EVER *AFTER.*

SOUND GOOD TO YOU?

LOIS, MY LOVE...

...WHAT DO *YOU* THINK?

The EnD...

59

INTERSTATE 55 BAKES IN THE OVEN OF NOON. THE HORIZON RIPPLING AND CHURNING AS IF VIEWED THROUGH BOILING WATER.

HE'S HEADING *SOUTH*.

A SICKLY TINGLING TRAVERSES HIS SCALP, SETTLING AT THE NAPE OF HIS NECK. HIS SHIRT, DAMP AND UNPLEASANT, STICKS TO HIS SHOULDER BLADES.

THE EYES THAT ONCE WATCHED QUARKS AT PLAY ARE SUNKEN, AND SHOT WITH RED.

HALLUCINATIONS CROWD THE PERIPHERY OF HIS VISION.

FOR AN INSTANT THE CAR IS STREAKING THROUGH A BLOOD-SOAKED FOREST, THE BLURRED FACES OF EXTINCT ANIMALS STARING FROM THE CRIMSON UNDERGROWTH...

...BUT ONLY FOR AN INSTANT.

SWERVING, HE BRUISES HIS KNEE ON THE UNDERSIDE OF THE DASH-BOARD, AND THE PAIN IS NO LONGER A NOVELTY TO HIM.

EEE EEEEEEEEEE

BESIDE HIM LIES THE FRAGMENT OF A SHATTERED WORLD.

BEFORE HIM LIES THE SUNSTRUCK HIGHWAY.

DAILY PLANET

THE MAN OF TOMORROW IS HEADING SOUTH TO DIE.

SUPERMAN and SWAMP THING

THE JUNGLE LINE

WRITER
ALAN MOORE
·
PENCILLER
RICK VEITCH
·
INKER
AL WILLIAMSON
·
LETTERER
COSTANZA
·
COLORIST
TATJANA WOOD
·
EDITOR
JULIUS SCHWARTZ

ONCE HE BATHED IN THE HEART OF THE SUN, CARELESS OF THE MILE-HIGH GEYSERS OF FLAME THAT SPAT AT HIM IN FRUSTRATED OUTRAGE.

NOW, FOR HIS IMPUDENCE, IT COOKS HIM BY DEGREES.

THE CAR IS FULL OF PEOPLE...

CLARK?

.. AND THEN IT ISN'T A CAR AT ALL.

CLARK, ARE YOU TAKING ALL THIS IN?

I--I THINK SO.

GOOD. THIS IS SO BORING I KEEP TUNING OUT AND MISSING THINGS.

THEY DIDN'T NEED TO SEND BOTH OF US TO COVER A CHUNK OF ROCK...

IN SUMMARY, THEN, LADIES AND GENTLEMEN

IN THESE DAYS WHEN REPORTS OF ALIEN CONTACT ARE COMMONPLACE, THIS METEORITE MAY NOT APPEAR SPECIAL.

IT ISN'T. WHAT'S GROWING UPON IT IS.

THERE IS A TINY PATCH OF LIVING FUNGUS THAT HAS SOMEHOW SURVIVED THE RIGORS OF SPACE.

IT ISN'T SPECTACULARLY BIG OR COLORFUL... IT'S A DULLISH RED, AND YOU'D NEED A MICROSCOPE TO EXAMINE IT PROPERLY...

3

64

HOWEVER...THIS *LIFE FORM* HAS SURVIVED *DECADES*... POSSIBLY *CENTURIES*... IN AN *ABSOLUTE FRIGID VACUUM.*

TO *SCIENCE,* THIS IS AN *UN-PRECEDENTED* DISCOVERY.

DOES ANYONE HAVE ANY *QUESTIONS?*

YES? MS. *LANG,* I BELIEVE?

DR. *EVERETT,* IS THIS FIND *REALLY* THAT IMPORTANT?

AFTER ALL, FOR OVER *TWENTY YEARS* WE'VE HAD A LIVING ALIEN *JUST* AS INDESTRUCTIBLE UPON OUR PLANET.

AHH. YOU'RE TALKING ABOUT *SUPERMAN.*

WELL, THE *DIFFERENCE* IS THAT UNLIKE THIS *FUNGUS, SUPERMAN* COULD NOT BE EXPECTED TO LIE STILL THROUGH-OUT WHAT MAY BE *YEARS OF THOROUGH RESEARCH.*

ANY *OTHER* QUESTIONS?

FROM *KRYPTON?*

4

HUH? WELL, OF *COURSE* HE'S FROM *KRYPTON.* *EVERYBODY* KNOWS THAT. UH, CLARK? ARE YOU *FEELING* OKAY?

I'M UH... I'M *FINE...*

JUST A LITTLE *WARM,* THAT'S ALL...

SHE HELPED HIM OUTSIDE, GLAD OF AN EXCUSE TO QUIT THE STUFFY *PRESS* CONFERENCE.

INSTITUTE FOR EXTRATERRESTRIAL STUDIES

FEIGNING DIZZINESS, HE SEARCHED THROUGH A MEMORY VAST ENOUGH TO HAVE EVERY CONCEIVABLE SHAPE OF SNOWFLAKE PRECISELY FILED...

...AND HE REMEMBERED.

REM-UL'S ALMANAC OF OLD KRYPTON...

PAGE... *417...* ENTRY 5,308...

OLD KRYPTONIAN NAME: *AVAREL LITHOTIS...*COMMON NAME: *BLOODMOREL...*

...NATIVE TO THE *SCARLET JUNGLE,* THE *BLOODMOREL* IS AN UNUSUAL AND DANGEROUS FUNGUS.

ITS PREFERRED *GROWTH MEDIUM* IS *BLOOD.* TO THIS END, ITS MICROSCOPIC *SPORES* PERMEATE THE SKIN AND THRIVE WITHIN THE *BLOODSTREAM ITSELF...*

"...CAUSING *FEVER,* BOUTS OF *INCAPACITATION,* *HALLUCINATIONS,* CHRONIC *OVEREXERTION...*

"...AND EVENTUALLY, IN *92%* OF ALL KNOWN CASES...

"...DEATH."

5

66

THE "BOUTS OF INCAPACITATION" STARTED THE DAY AFTER THE PRESS CONFERENCE...

CLARK, *HONESTLY*, YOU'RE LIKE A LITTLE *KID!* IT'S ONLY A *PAPER CUT!* IT'S HARDLY BLEEDING AT *ALL!*

IT TOOK HIS INVULNERABILITY AN HOUR TO RETURN.

HE TESTED IT EVERY TEN MINUTES, HOLDING HIS HAND UNDER THE HOT FAUCET IN THE WASHROOM UNTIL THERE WAS NO PAIN.

SHORTLY AFTER LUNCH HE DISCOVERED THAT HE COULD NO LONGER SEE THROUGH SOLID OBJECTS OR HEAR AT A DISTANCE.

JEEZ, KENT! *KNOCK,* WHYDONCHA?

OH, I'M, UH... I'M SORRY...

BY SIX O'CLOCK, HIS X-RAY VISION HAD RETURNED, ALTHOUGH HIS EARS STILL FELT STUFFED WITH COTTON.

HE CONSIDERED FLYING TO HIS APARTMENT...

...BUT DECIDED AGAINST IT AND TOOK THE *SUBWAY* INSTEAD.

RRHOIDS? PAINFUL SWELLING

6

HIS SUPER-HEARING RETURNED, DEAFENINGLY, WHILE HE WAS CROSSING SEVENTH AVENUE ON HIS WAY TO WORK.

THERE WAS ONLY ONE OPTION OPEN TO HIM.

INSTITUTE FOR EXTRA-TERRESTRIAL STUDIES

TOUCHINGLY, DR. EVERETT HAD GIVEN HIM THE PROMISED METEORITE ALMOST WITHOUT QUESTION.

LATER, DURING COFFEE BREAK, HE KNOCKED A CUP FROM HIS DESK AND WASN'T FAST ENOUGH TO CATCH IT.

HE PROMISED TO RETURN IT, UNHARMED, IF THAT WAS POSSIBLE.

RETURNING TO HIS APARTMENT, HE BEGAN TO EXAMINE IT FOR CLUES TO A POSSIBLE ANTIDOTE.

AFTER TWENTY MINUTES, HIS MICROSCOPIC VISION FAILED AND HE WAS FORCED TO STOP.

HE UNDERSTOOD THEN THAT HE WAS GOING TO DIE...

...AND THE ONLY QUESTION THAT REMAINED WAS WHERE.

8

HE WANTED TO BE *ALONE* WHEN IT HAPPENED, BUT HIS *FORTRESS* WAS TOO DISTANT, AND FLYING WAS *UNTHINKABLE.*

COAST CITY

CENTRAL CITY

STAR CITY

HE ALSO ELIMINATED GOTHAM, NEW YORK, WASHINGTON, AND ALL OTHER CITIES FREQUENTED BY THE SUPER-HERO COMMUNITY!

*F*INALLY, HE BOUGHT A SECONDHAND CAR IN A CASH TRANSACTION UNDER THE NAME OF CAL ELLIS.

SUPER DEALS

AL'S USED CARS

TAKING THE *METEORITE,* JUST IN CASE, HE MADE FOR THE ONE PLACE IN AMERICA WITH NO INDIGENOUS SUPERHUMANS...

HE HEADED SOUTH.

BLAAAAAAA

HHROON

9

70

72

KAL-EL?

IT'S NO GOOD *RUNNING,* KAL-EL...

YOU'VE BEEN RUNNING FOR MORE THAN *TWENTY YEARS,* KAL-EL...

...RUNNING FROM THE DEATH OF YOUR *PLANET.*

YOU SHOULD HAVE *DIED* ON *KRYPTON,* KAL-EL, AS YOU WERE *MEANT* TO. YOU *KNOW* THAT, DON'T YOU?

NOW, AFTER ALL THESE YEARS OF *RUNNING,* YOUR *DESTINY* HAS FINALLY *CAUGHT UP* WITH YOU...

HERE, KAL-EL...

HERE IN THE *SCARLET JUNGLE.*

LEAVE ME ALONE!

YOU'RE ALL **DEAD!**

EXTINCT IS THE WORD, KAL-EL.

WE'RE *EXTINCT,* LIKE *ALL* KRYPTONIANS...

COME AND *JOIN* US. TAKE YOUR PLACE IN THE SHADE OF THESE BROAD CRIMSON LEAVES...

...**FOREVER!**

/2

HIS FACE...IS STRANGELY... FAMILIAR...

SLEEPING...HE CLASPS THE ROCK...TO HIS BREAST... AS IF IT WERE... AN UGLY CHILD...

I EXAMINE IT...

ITS UNDERSIDE...IS DISCOLORED ...BY BRITTLE PINK MOSS...A SPECIES...THAT I DO NOT...RECOGNIZE...

INQUISITIVE... I BRUSH...ITS DRY AND ENGRAVED SURFACE... WITH MY FINGERTIPS...

I SENSE...THE UNUSUAL RHYTHMS...IN ITS CELLS... IN ITS PARCHED TISSUES...

CONCENTRATING... I TRY... TO ESTABLISH...

...CONTACT.

RED TREES...RED SUN... TOO MUCH GRAVITY...TOO MUCH SENSATION...

PULL BACK...PULL BACK AWAY FROM IT...

THE STONE DROPS ...FROM MY FINGERS... AND THE CONTACT... IS BROKEN...

WHAT HAPPENED?

I...TOUCHED IT... AND I WAS ON... ANOTHER WORLD...

IT ISN'T...FROM HERE. IT'S... FOREIGN...

...ALIEN.

13

I STUDY THE MAN'S FACE... ITS HAUNTING FAMILIARITY...

STAY *BACK!* ALL OF YOU! STAY *BACK* FROM ME!

I BEGIN TO OPEN... THE BLACKENED TATTERS ...OF HIS SHIRT...

I *WON'T* ROT HERE WITH THE REST OF YOU! YOU CAN'T *KEEP* ME HERE!

I THINK... THAT I KNOW... WHO HE *IS*...

I MOVE TOWARDS HIM.

HE MOVED SLIGHTLY... MUTTERING WORDS... IN ANOTHER LANGUAGE...

I DON'T *BELONG* HERE! I'M NOT *DEAD*...

DON'T YOU KNOW WHO I *AM?*

SUPERMAN?

UNHH... GET AWAY... YOU'RE ALL *DEAD*...

GET AWAY FROM ME!!

14

NOOOO!

SsZZ||ZZT!

PLEASE... YOU CANNOT... DESTROY ME...

I AM A... FRIEND...

YOU MUST NOT... *EXERT* YOURSELF...

YOU WON'T TRICK ME *THAT* WAY. YOU WANT ME TO *GIVE UP*, IS *THAT* IT?

WELL, IT WON'T *WORK*...

I'M *SUPERMAN*.

I GO DOWN **FIGHTING!**

SHRUNCH!

NO...

IT IS... THE FIGHTING... THAT IS KILLING YOU...

YOU...ARE *BURNING* UP...FROM THE *INSIDE*...

THE FEVER...*RAGING* WITHIN YOU...*PUSHES*... YOUR WEAKENED BODY... BEYOND ITS *LIMITS*...

LIMITS... YES! YES, I...

...I *REMEMBER*...

"*CHRONIC OVEREXERTION,* AND EVENTUALLY... EVENTUALLY..."

"...*EVENTUALLY*... *DEATH.*"

YOU MUST...BE *STILL*...IF YOU WISH...TO *SURVIVE*...

I *CAN'T*... THE *FEVER*... *SCARLET JUNGLE* FEVER...I'M SO *HOT*...

FORGET... THE *SCARLET*... AND THE *HEAT*...

TOUCH MY *HAND*... AND LET... THE *INFERNO* WITHIN YOU BE... *EXTINGUISHED*...

"...BY COOL *DARKNESS*..."

"...BY *ENDLESS GREEN*..."

20

DAYLIGHT.

A PALE SUN CLIMBS ABOVE THE GRAY TREES.

HE IS ALIVE.

STRUGGLING TO HIS FEET, HE CHECKS HIMSELF.

THERE IS NO PAIN. LOOKING BENEATH HIS SKIN, HE CAN SEE NO BROKEN BONES, NO HOSTILE ORGANISMS THRIVING WITHIN HIS BLOOD.

IN WASHINGTON, A CONGRESSMAN'S WIFE CLEARS HER THROAT AND HE HEARS IT.

IN HARLEM, A BABY WAKES UP CRYING, AND HE HEARS IT.

THE FEVER AND THE WEAKNESS HAVE PASSED.

HE IS SUPERMAN.

HE WONDERS ABOUT THE ROCK. HAD ITS COURSE FROM THE EXPLODED PLANET AVOIDED THE RADIATION BELT THAT WOULD HAVE TRANSFORMED IT TO KRYPTONITE?

NO MATTER. HE KNOWS THAT IT CANNOT HARM HIM NOW.

HE SURVIVED.

LAUNCHING HIMSELF UPWARDS, THE HALF-REMEMBERED FEVER-DREAMS OF THE NIGHT BEFORE DROP AWAY FROM HIM

HE SURVIVED...

22

SURVIVED, WHEN THERE WAS NO HOPE OF ANOTHER MORNING AS GLORIOUS AS THIS ONE...

SURVIVED, WHEN THERE WAS NO ONE THERE TO HELP HIM.

UPWIND, THERE IS A SPLASH AS A 'GATOR THRASHES ITS TAIL, NOSING OUT INTO THE DEEP WATER.

...THE VINE-DRAPED SHADOWS BECKON.

THE ANCIENT TREES WHISPER...

THEIR LEAVES ARE A BURNISHED CRIMSON IN THE FIRST SHAFTS OF DAWN...

PROLOGUE

WEST OF THE CITY, RED EVENING LIGHT REFRACTS THROUGH GIANT MESAS OF DIAMOND. THE SKY RIPPLES AT THE HORIZON, PASTEL VEILS BILLOWING IN THE WIND.

WALKING HOME, WEARY, THE SPECTACLE IS LOST UPON HIM.

WORKING AT THE INSTITUTE OF GEOLOGY SINCE DAWN, HE HAS CATALOGUED TWO HUNDRED SPECIMENS FROM THE KANDOR CRATER.

EYES ACHING, HE WONDERS IF VAN AND ORNA WILL STILL BE UP.

THE MUFFLED BLARE OF THE HOLOFACTOR COMES FROM THE FOREROOM, WHERE THE CHILDREN WATCH "NIGHTWING AND FLAMEBIRD." GOOD. THEY'RE AWAKE.

HE'LL READ THEM ANOTHER "SCARLET JUNGLE" STORY BEFORE BED, LEAVING THE NIGHT FOR HIM AND LYLA...

...JUST THE TWO OF THEM.

SURPRISE! YOU DIDN'T **HEAR** US, FATHER...

HAPPY FIRSTDAY, KAL...

VAN TUGS AT HIS TUNIC, AND **KARA ZOR-EL** GIVES HIM A NEW HEADBAND. ON THE HOLOFACTOR, NIGHTWING SAVES FLAMEBIRD FROM A ROGUE METAL-EATER.

HIS WEARINESS LIFTS. THE MAN HAS HIS FAMILY ABOUT HIM.

HE IS CONTENT.

1

THE ARCTIC CIRCLE, FEBRUARY 29TH:

BEAT YOU.

IF I EVER DEVELOP A BAT-PLANE THAT RESPONDS TO *THOUGHT-CONTROL*, I'LL TAKE YOU UP ON A REMATCH.

IT'S GOOD TO SEE YOU AGAIN, DIANA. YOU'RE LOOKING GREAT.

OH, THIS IS *JASON TODD...*

OH, OF *COURSE*, THE NEW *ROBIN*. I'M SORRY, JASON ... YOU LOOK SO MUCH LIKE *DICK* THAT I FORGOT FOR A MOMENT...

NICE TO MEET YOU. WELCOME TO AN INTERESTING CAREER.

ANYWAY, HE'S LEFT THE DOOR OPEN FOR US. LET'S GET *INSIDE* BEFORE YOU TWO *FREEZE*.

BEFORE *US* TWO FREEZE? DRESSED LIKE *THAT*?

THINK CLEAN THOUGHTS, CHUM.

EVERY TIME I COME HERE, THAT ICE SLOPE UP TO THE ENTRANCE GETS *STEEPER*. I WISH SOMEONE WOULD TELL HIM THAT NOT *EVERYONE* CAN FLY.

IS THIS YOUR FIRST VISIT TO THE FORTRESS, JASON?

UH, YEAH.

I MEAN, I MET *SUPERMAN* BEFORE, BUT I STILL DON'T REALLY, UH, *KNOW* HIM THAT WELL.

THIS IS A BIG PLACE, ISN'T IT? I BET THERE'S SOME SCARY STUFF IN HERE....

WELL, IF YOU MAKE A *PROFESSION* OUT OF THAT *MASK*, YOU'LL PROBABLY SEE A LOT *WORSE*.

INCIDENTALLY, DIANA, WHAT KIND OF PRESENT DID YOU DECIDE TO GET HIM?

I'M NOT SAYING *ANYTHING*. HE'LL *HEAR* AND IT'LL SPOIL THE *SURPRISE*.

HEAR? BUT HE'S NOT EVEN ANYWHERE NEAR US. HE WON'T...

OH. OH, RIGHT. SUPERMAN. I FORGOT.

CHOOSING GIFTS FOR HIM IS *ALWAYS* DIFFICULT.

THIS YEAR, I PAID A *HORTICULTURALIST* TO BREED A NEW STRAIN OF *ROSE* CALLED "THE KRYPTON." I'M PRETTY CERTAIN NO ONE ELSE WILL HAVE GOT HIM FLOWERS...

UH, BRUCE...

MAYBE IT'S NOT TOO LATE TO CHANGE IT FOR SOMETHING *ELSE*.

DID YOU GET A *RECEIPT*?

3

WHAT **IS** IT? IT LOOKS LIKE IT'S GROWING **INTO** HIM, THROUGH HIS **COSTUME**...

BUT...

...BUT HE'S **SUPERMAN**.

IS HE **BREATHING**?

YES. YES, BUT VERY **FAINTLY**.

BRUCE, THIS THING FEELS **FUNNY**. I THINK IT MIGHT HAVE SOME **MAGIC** IN IT...

IF IT'S **GROWING** THROUGH THE **COSTUME**, THAT WOULD MAKE **SENSE**. IT LOOKS LIKE HE WAS OPENING A **GIFT**...

BRUCE, LISTEN, IF SOMETHING'S DONE **THIS** TO SUPERMAN...

...THEN WE HAVE TO FIND OUT WHAT IT IS AS QUICKLY AS POSSIBLE WITHOUT WASTING TIME **WORRYING**.

CHECK THOSE WRAPPINGS THOROUGHLY ...AND BE **CAREFUL**.

I DON'T THINK WE SHOULD TRY **REMOVING** IT. IF IT'S GROWING **INTO** HIM...

NO. YOU'RE RIGHT.

HIS PUPILS AREN'T CONTRACTING EVEN **SLIGHTLY**. HE MUST BE CUT OFF FROM JUST ABOUT ALL SENSATION...

HE'S IN A WORLD OF HIS **OWN**.

5

KAL?

WHY ARE YOU STILL STARING OUT OF THE WINDOW? THE UNDERLIGHTS OF AUNT ALLURA'S *PARAGONDOLA* VANISHED FIVE UNITS AGO.

EVERY-ONE'S GONE *HOME*.

NO REASON.

IT'S JUST THAT...

WELL, IT WOULD HAVE BEEN NICE IF MY *FATHER* HAD BEEN HERE TONIGHT...

WELL, I *INVITED* HIM, BUT WHEN I TOLD HIM *ALLURA* AND *KARA* WOULD BE HERE, HE SAID HE WAS *BUSY*.

HE'S SO *UNREASONABLE*, KAL. I KNOW HE *ARGUED* WITH HIS BROTHER, BUT *ZOR-EL'S* BEEN DEAD FOR THREE *YEARS* NOW...

...AND MY FATHER *STILL* WON'T SPEAK TO ALLURA OR KARA. I KNOW. IT'S *STUPID*.

A STUPID ARGUMENT OVER *POLITICS*.

YES, WELL, IT ISN'T EXACTLY *DIFFICULT* TO ARGUE OVER POLITICS WITH *JOR-EL* THESE DAYS...

WHY NOT *VISIT* HIM TOMORROW, AFTER *WORK*? JUST DON'T WORRY ABOUT HIM *TONIGHT*. IT'S YOUR *FIRSTDAY*.

THE *RO-BUTLERS* WILL CLEAR UP. LET'S GO TO BED.

LYLA, WHY DID YOU EVER GIVE UP *ACTING* FOR *THIS*?

I DON'T KNOW, KAL.

REMIND ME.

KAL, LOR-EM HAS A LOT OF **PEOPLE** BEHIND HIM. PEOPLE WITH **INFLUENCE.**

IF THE **OLD KRYPTON MOVEMENT** IS TO HAVE **ANY** POLITICAL STRENGTH IN THE CHAMBERS...

OLD KRYPTON MOVEMENT? YOU'RE REALLY GOING THROUGH WITH THAT?

SOMEONE HAS TO.

LOOK AROUND YOU, KAL. WHAT'S **HAPPENED** TO KRYPTON? THERE'S THE DRUG TRAFFIC IN **GLAMOR-SALTS** AND **HELLBLOSSOM** COMING IN FROM **ERKOL**...

THERE'S RACIAL TROUBLE WITH THE VATHLO ISLAND IMMIGRANTS...

FATHER, KRYPTON IS **CHANGING,** AND THE CHANGE IS **DIFFICULT.** EXTREMIST POLITICAL GROUPS AREN'T MAKING IT ANY **EASIER**...

...AND GRUBBING FOR ROCKS IN THE KANDOR CRATER IS, I SUPPOSE?

I HAD GREAT **HOPES** FOR YOU, KAL...

THAT ISN'T **FAIR**...

WELL? WHEN HAS ANYONE EVER BEEN FAIR TO **ME?** WAS IT **FAIR** THAT I WAS FORCED TO RESIGN FROM THE SCIENCE COUNCIL?

WAS IT **FAIR** THAT THE **EATING SICKNESS** TOOK YOUR MOTHER?

THAT WAS **TWENTY YEARS** AGO. I **KNOW** THE SCIENCE COUNCIL TREATED YOU **BADLY,** BUT...

BADLY? THEY IMPLIED THAT I WAS **INSANE!**

ALL RIGHT, SO MY THEORY WAS **INCORRECT.** I BELIEVED KRYPTON WAS **DOOMED** AND I WAS **WRONG**...

DOES THAT GIVE THEM THE RIGHT TO PUSH ME **ASIDE,** AND LET SOCIETY FALL TO **PIECES?**

YOU KNOW, I HEAR THEY'RE CAMPAIGNING TO RELEASE THE **PHANTOM ZONE** CRIMINALS. "UNREASONABLY **SEVERE** PUNISHMENT," THEY CALL IT...

FATHER...

8

SOMETIMES, I THINK YOU WISH YOU WERE *RIGHT.*

I THINK YOU WISH KRYPTON *HAD* EXPLODED AFTER ALL.

I HAVE TO GO NOW.

CHRIIISSSSHH

"REALLY, IT'S JUST A MATTER OF PUTTING THE PIECES *TOGETHER...*"

I THINK IT'S SAFE TO ASSUME FROM THOSE *WRAPPINGS* THAT SUPERMAN RECEIVED THIS THING AS A *GIFT*...

...BUT *HOW?*

I GUESS THE *U.S. MAIL* DOESN'T *REACH* THIS FAR...

LISTEN, IT HAS TO BE *ALIEN* IN ORIGIN. I KNOW THAT A LOT OF ALIEN CULTURES SEND HIM *GIFTS*...

HMM. I SUPPOSE HE MUST HAVE A *TELE-PORTATION CHANNEL,* ALTHOUGH HE'S NEVER MENTIONED ONE...

PERHAPS HE DOESN'T *USE* THE CHANNEL OFTEN... JUST ONCE A YEAR, WHEN IT'S HIS *BIRTH-DAY...*

IT'S *POSSIBLE* ...

SOME *GRATEFUL* WORLD MAY HAVE SENT THIS AS A *GIFT,* UNAWARE THAT IT COULD *HARM* HIM ...

HOW *REMARKABLE.* YOU ANIMALS REALLY ARE ALMOST *INTELLIGENT,* AREN'T YOU?

THAT'S *EXACTLY* WHAT HAPPENED...

...EXCEPT FOR ONE OR TWO *MINOR* DETAILS.

FIRSTLY, I KNEW *PRECISELY* WHAT IT WOULD DO TO HIM.

SECONDLY, IT WAS NOT INTENDED AS A TOKEN OF *GRATITUDE*.

WHAT *IS* IT?

I DON'T KNOW. START TO MOVE AWAY SLOWLY. PERHAPS WE CAN PLAY FOR *TIME* ...

UH, WHAT EXACTLY *IS* THAT CREATURE?

DO YOU *LIKE* IT?

IT'S CALLED A "*BLACK MERCY.*" I TRAVELED A GREAT WAY INTO THE *TANGLED ZONES* TO LOCATE IT.

...OH, AND *PLEASE* TELL THE LITTLE YELLOW CREATURE TO STOP *SHUFFLING*. IT DISTRACTS ME.

IT'S SOMETHING BETWEEN A *PLANT* AND AN INTELLIGENT *FUNGUS*. IT ATTACHES ITSELF TO ITS VICTIMS IN A FORM OF *SYMBIOSIS*, FEEDING FROM THEIR *BIO-AURA*.

AND WHAT DOES IT DO FOR THEM IN *RETURN*?

WHY, IT GIVES THEM THEIR *HEART'S DESIRE*.

I'D SAY THAT WAS *FAIR*, WOULDN'T YOU?

IT'S *TELEPATHIC*. IT READS THEM LIKE A *BOOK*, AND IT FEEDS THEM A *LOGICAL SIMULATION* OF THE HAPPY ENDING THEY *DESIRE*.

OF COURSE, ITS VICTIMS *COULD* SHRUG IT OFF...

THEY JUST *DON'T* WANT TO.

11

I *DELIVERED* IT TO HIM, AND WHEN I WAS *CERTAIN* THAT IT HAD DONE ITS *WORK,* I FOLLOWED IT ALONG THE *TELEPORTATION CHANNEL.*

POOR LITTLE CREATURE, I WONDER WHERE HE THINKS HE *IS?*

PERHAPS HE'S PLAYING HAPPILY AS A CHILD IN WHATEVER SORDID ABORIGINAL *BACK-WATER* HE WAS *RAISED* IN, OR BOUNCING ON HIS MOTHER'S *KNEE...*

THAT WOULD BE *NICE,* WOULDN'T IT? TO THINK OF HIM, CAREFREE AND CONTENTED...

FOREVER.

WHAT... *ARE...* YOU?

IF YOU DON'T ALREADY *KNOW* MY NAME, THEN YOU'RE NOT WORTHY OF AN *INTRODUCTION.*

I'M THE NEW *MANAGER* AROUND HERE.

NATURALLY, I SHALL NEED TIME TO *SETTLE* IN AND ADJUST TO YOUR MANY INTERESTING *CUSTOMS...*

I KNOW, FOR EXAMPLE, THAT YOUR SOCIETY MAKES *DISTINCTIONS* ON A BASIS OF *GENDER* AND *AGE.*

PERHAPS, THEN, YOU COULD *ADVISE* ME...

WHICH OF YOU WOULD IT BE POLITE TO KILL *FIRST?*

12

WELL?

THRUTCH

HMM...

AAAK...

THANK YOU.

I THINK THAT'S ANSWERED MY QUESTION

13

"JAX-UR: MORE THAN TWENTY YEARS IN LIMBO ...JUST BECAUSE IT DOESN'T HURT, THAT DOESN'T MEAN IT ISN'T TORTURE...FREE PHANTOM ZONE EXILES NOW..."

I--I'VE SEEN THESE THINGS AROUND, BUT...

THE *ANTI-PHANTOM ZONE* CAMPAIGNERS SEE THE PHANTOM ZONE RAY AS AN INSTRUMENT OF *TORTURE*. YOUR FATHER *INVENTED* IT.

THAT MAKES THE *HOUSE OF EL* UNPOPULAR IN CERTAIN QUARTERS, AS YOUR COUSIN *DISCOVERED.*

SHE'S THROUGH HERE. PERHAPS, NURSE, YOU COULD ENTERTAIN THE *CHILD...?*

OF COURSE.

HELLO. MY NAME'S *ANSULA.* WHAT'S *YOURS?*

VAN.

VAN-*EL.*

KARA?

PLEASE... ONLY A FEW MOMENTS. SHE'S VERY *WEAK...*

"EVERYTHING'S *FINE*."

WELL, YOU'RE CERTAINLY LASTING LONGER THAN I ANTICIPATED.

YOU'RE A *FEMALE*, I THINK. YOU WOULDN'T BE THE KRYPTONIAN'S *MATE*, BY ANY CHANCE?

JUST... *GOOD*... FRIENDS...

LET'S *SEE*... IF WE *CAN*... EVEN UP THE *ODDS*... A LITTLE...

OH, DEAR. IS THAT A *NEURAL IMPACTER*? DO THEY STILL MAKE THOSE?

I'D ADVISE YOU TO TRY THE *PLASM DISRUPTER*. IT'S *SMALLER*.

MORE OF A *FEMALE'S* WEAPON.

GO TO HELL!

KA-CHIK

18

BRUCE... THAT *EXPLOSION*...

HE KNOCKED HER THROUGH THE FAR *WALL*, AND, AND...

BRUCE, WHAT'S *HAPPENING* IN THERE?

IF WE'RE *LUCKY*, THAT EXPLOSION MEANS DIANA'S FOUND THE *HALL OF WEAPONS*.

WE'VE GOT TO CONCENTRATE ON REVIVING *SUPERMAN*...

...BECAUSE WHATEVER'S GOING ON THROUGH THERE IS WAY OUT OF OUR *LEAGUE*.

SUPERMAN? KAL? WE'RE IN SERIOUS TROUBLE, OLD FRIEND. YOU'VE GOT TO WAKE UP.

THAT'S *ALL*, KAL...

JUST *WAKE UP*...

19

...OFF?

BRUCE!

BRUCE, LOOK OUT! IT'S...

THEY ARE IN THE DARK AND FAMILIAR STREETS OF OLD GOTHAM, WALKING HOME AFTER THE SHOW...

THERE IS THE SOUND OF HIS FATHER'S LAUGHTER, THE SMELL OF HIS MOTHER'S PERFUME...

OH, NO!

BRUCE? BRUCE, DON'T LET IT GET HOLD OF YOU...

...AND THEN THE MAN WITH THE WEASEL FACE STEPS FROM THE SHADOWS, CARRYING AN UGLY-LOOKING GUN...

...AND HE FIRES...

BRUCE?

...AND HE MISSES...

...AND THOMAS WAYNE TAKES THE GUN AWAY FROM HIM WITH NO TROUBLE AT ALL.

24

OH, *NO*. I CAN'T *HANDLE* THIS.

BRUCE, WAKE *UP*...

THE POLICE LEAD THE MAN AWAY AND THE CHILD IS SAFE IN HIS MOTHER'S ARMS.

THE DARK CLOUD OF TERROR THAT HAD FLAPPED SQUEAKING THROUGH HIS MIND BREAKS UP, DISPERSING FOREVER.

HE IS CONTENT.

PLEASE. PLEASE WAKE UP. I DON'T KNOW IF A *HUMAN* BODY CAN *STAND* CONTACT WITH THIS JUNK, EVEN IF IT *DIDN'T* DO ANY HARM TO...

...SUPERMAN.

WHO... DID *THIS*...TO *ME*?

I ...I DON'T KNOW.

A BIG YELLOW GUY. HE'S THROUGH THERE HURTING WONDER WOMAN NOW ...

SUPERMAN? ARE YOU OKAY? YOU LOOK SORTA, UH...

MONGUL ...

SUPERMAN! WAIT...

FFWOOSH

HE HEARS A VOICE LIKE ARMAGEDDON SHOUTING HIS NAME, AND HE STARTS TO TURN...

HE KNOWS HE HAS PERHAPS LESS THAN HALF A SECOND IN WHICH TO DEFEND HIMSELF...

26

WHAT AM I GOING TO DO ABOUT *BRUCE?* I CAN'T...

UH...

HE STARTS TO REACH TOWARDS HIS ARMOR'S WEAPON SYSTEMS, LETTING THE UNCONSCIOUS WOMAN CRUMPLE TO THE FLOOR...

...BUT THE ROCK OF THE FAR WALL SEEMS TO RIPPLE OUTWARDS IN A SUDDEN CASCADE OF POWDER...

...AND A FOUR-HUNDRED-MILE-AN-HOUR WIND SLAMS INTO HIM LIKE A STEAM HAMMER AS BIG AS THE *WORLD*...

...AND HE KNOWS THAT HE IS FAR TOO LATE.

27

EUGH...

GET UP.

GET *UP*, YOU VERMIN!

DO YOU UNDER-STAND WHAT YOU *DID* TO ME?

PERFECTLY.

28

AAAAAAAA

THEY'RE UP *THERE*? HOW AM I GONNA GET UP THERE WITH *THIS* THING?

THERE AREN'T ANY STAIRS IN THIS PLACE AND THERE'S NOWHERE I CAN PUT IT, AND...

HMMM.

30

EYES SPIT OUT SUNS. MUSCLES SHIFT LIKE CONTINENTAL PLATES, ROILING UNDER A HIDE OF JAUNDICED LEATHER ...

BECOMING OVER-EXCITED, THREE SENTIENT PUDDLES FROM MINRAUD IV EVAPORATE COMPLETELY, LEAVING A FAINT ODOR OF GASOLINE.

IN THE CHAMBER OF ARCHIVES, A MACHINE WITH A BRAIN MADE OF LIGHT IS COUNTING THE DISTANT PULSARS.

WITHIN TEN FEET OF ITS ALGEBRAIC REVERIE, ALIEN ENGINES OF FURY GRIND TOGETHER UNNOTICED.

THEIR ENMITY CAN ONLY BE MEASURED IN THE SKIPPED HEART-BEATS OF DISTANT SEISMOGRAPHS.

BOTH INDESTRUCTIBLE, EACH DAMAGES THE OTHER.

BOTH IRRESISTIBLE, EACH FINDS HIM-SELF THWARTED ...

SURRENDER IS NOT A POSSIBILITY.

32

117

KRYPTON...?

THERE...

DO YOU KNOW, I ALMOST BELIEVED THAT YOU WERE GOING TO KILL ME.

HOW STUPID OF YOU TO HESITATE LIKE THAT...

NOT A MISTAKE THAT I'LL MAKE, I ASSURE YOU...

UH, EXCUSE ME...

34

...AND HE SWATS THE THING ASIDE, REDUCING THE BOY TO ASH WITH THE TWITCH OF A CIRCUIT...

...AND THEN HE RIPS THE KRYPTONIAN'S HEAD FROM HIS SHOULDERS, LAUGHING AT THE WAY THAT THE EYES ROLL FOR LONG SECONDS AFTER DEATH...

...AND THEN HE PLACES IT UPON A SPIKE AND GOES OUT TO TRAMPLE A WORLD, CARRYING IT BEFORE HIM, HIS HIDEOUS STANDARD.

IT'S OVER.

36

LATER:

HOW DO YOU FEEL?

STILL A LITTLE SHAKY. IT WAS SO STRANGE... I WAS MARRIED TO KATHY KANE AND WE HAD A TEENAGED DAUGHTER...

I'M A LITTLE ENVIOUS. IT MUST BE WONDERFUL TO FIND OUT JUST WHAT YOUR HEART'S DESIRE REALLY IS.

MONGUL LOOKS LIKE HE'S HAVING A PRETTY GOOD TIME.

WHAT WILL YOU DO WITH HIM SUPERMAN?

I'M GOING TO PUT HIM SOMEWHERE SECURE.

WHAT, YOU MEAN BUILD A PRISON, OR ..?

NOT EXACTLY. HAVE YOU EVER NOTICED THAT BLACK HOLE AS YOU COME IN VIA THE WESTERN SPIRAL ARM OF THE GALAXY?

UH, NO. NO, I CAN'T SAY THAT I HAVE...

IT'S QUITE LARGE. I THINK I'LL DROP HIM INTO IT.

KAL? NOW THAT WE'VE BROKEN THE ICE AT YOUR BIRTH-DAY PARTY, CAN I GIVE YOU THIS?

IT'S AN EXACT DUPLICATE OF THE BOTTLE CITY OF KANDOR, TO REPLACE THE REAL ONE, WHICH WAS ENLARGED.

THE PARADISE ISLAND GEM-SMITHS MADE IT. YOU NEED X-RAY AND MICROSCOPIC VISION TO REALLY APPRECIATE IT...

OH.

UH...

WHY, DIANA, THAT'S...

37

122

...WHAT I'VE ALWAYS WANTED.

I'M GLAD. YOU MUST HAVE MISSED THE OLD ONE.

HAPPY BIRTHDAY, KAL.

MMM. WHY DON'T WE DO THAT MORE OFTEN?

I DON'T KNOW. TOO PREDICTABLE?

YOU'RE PROBABLY RIGHT.

JASON AND I BROUGHT YOU THIS NEW BREED OF ROSE, NAMED "THE KRYPTON," BUT, UH...

WELL, I'M AFRAID IT GOT STEPPED ON, AND...

WELL FRANKLY, IT'S DEAD.

DON'T WORRY ABOUT IT, BRUCE.

PERHAPS IT'S FOR THE BEST.

COME ON...

DOES SOMEBODY WANT TO MAKE COFFEE WHILE I CLEAN THE PLACE UP?

39

ALAN MOORE is perhaps the most acclaimed writer in the graphic story medium, having garnered countless awards for works such as WATCHMEN, V FOR VENDETTA, *From Hell, Miracleman* and SWAMP THING. He is also the mastermind behind the America's Best Comics line, through which he has created (along with many talented illustrators) THE LEAGUE OF EXTRAORDINARY GENTLEMEN, PROMETHEA, TOM STRONG, TOMORROW STORIES and TOP 10. As one of the medium's most important innovators since the early 1980s, Moore has influenced an entire generation of comics creators, and his work continues to inspire an ever-growing audience. Moore resides in central England.

CURT SWAN entered the art field intending to become not a cartoonist but a "slick" magazine illustrator like Norman Rockwell or Joseph Leyendecker. While serving during World War II illustrating the Army newspaper *Stars and Stripes*, Swan worked with DC writer France E. Herron. On Herron's suggestion, Swan found work at DC after the war. Swan's versatile pencils, which he remembers applying first to BOY COMMANDOS, soon appeared on various DC features, including Superman, Batman, the Newsboy Legion, Big Town, Mr. District Attorney, Tommy Tomorrow, and Swan's longest assignment up to that time, Superboy. His familiarity with both Superman and Batman specially suited him to draw the original Superman-Batman team-up in 1952. Swan served various stints, regular and semi-regular, on almost all the Superman titles of the 1950s and 1960s, and remained the near-exclusive Superman penciller throughout the 1970s and much of the 1980s. Although he "retired" in 1986, Swan continued to work for DC until his death in 1996. To generations of professionals and fans, Curt Swan's Superman will always be the definitive version.

DAVE GIBBONS has worked in comics since 1973. Cutting his teeth on underground comics and fanzines, he became a frequent contributor to the UK anthology magazine *2000 AD*, illustrating such features as Harlem Heroes, Dan Dare and Rogue Trooper (which he co-created), as well as providing work to *Doctor Who Magazine*. In 1982 he landed an assignment on GREEN LANTERN, beginning his long association with DC Comics. Since then he has both drawn and written many of their major characters, including Superman and Batman. In 1986 Gibbons and writer Alan Moore co-created the landmark series WATCHMEN, which is widely acknowledged to be one of the greatest graphic narratives ever published. Since then, he has collaborated with a wide variety of writers and artists, including Frank Miller (*Give Me Liberty, Martha Washington Goes to War*), Garth Ennis (WAR STORY: SCREAMING EAGLES) and Geoff Johns (GREEN LANTERN CORPS: RECHARGE), and in 2005 his Vertigo graphic novel THE ORIGINALS won the Eisner Award for Best New Graphic Album.

RICK VEITCH worked in the underground comics scene before attending the Joe Kubert School of Cartoon and Graphic Art. After graduating, he worked with Stephen Bissette on *Bizarre Adventures* before creating and illustrating *The One*, the innovative Epic Comics miniseries. In addition to writing and drawing an acclaimed run on SWAMP THING, he is the creator/cartoonist of *Brat Pack, Maximortal* and the dream-based *Rare Bit Fiends*, and a contributing artist on *1963*. He is also the writer and artist of the miniseries *Greyshirt: Indigo Sunset* from America's Best Comics, and the creator of the critically acclaimed graphic novel CAN'T GET NO and the spectacularly satirical series ARMY@LOVE from Vertigo.

GEORGE PÉREZ started drawing at the age of five and hasn't stopped since. Born on June 9, 1954, Pérez began his professional comics career as an assistant to Rich Buckler in 1973. After establishing himself as a penciller at Marvel Comics, Pérez came to DC in 1980, bringing his highly detailed art style to such titles as JUSTICE LEAGUE OF AMERICA and FIRESTORM. After co-creating THE NEW TEEN TITANS in 1980, Pérez and writer Marv Wolfman reunited for the landmark miniseries CRISIS ON INFINITE EARTHS in 1985. In the aftermath of that universe-smashing event, Pérez revitalized WONDER WOMAN as the series' writer and artist, reestablishing her as one of DC's most preeminent characters and bringing in some of the best sales the title has ever experienced. He has since gone on to illustrate celebrated runs on Marvel's *The Avengers*, CrossGen's *Solus* and DC's THE BRAVE AND THE BOLD.

KURT SCHAFFENBERGER began his comics career in 1941 as a member of the Binder brothers shop, illustrating a number of different features for numerous publishers. His best-loved work, however, was for Fawcett Comics — the home of the original Captain Marvel and the Marvel Family. Besides the Big Red Cheese, Schaffenberger also drew the adventures of Bulletman, Ibis, Spy Smasher, Mr. Scarlet and Golden Arrow for Fawcett until the company's demise in 1953. In demand for romance comics because of his ultra-smooth line, Schaffenberger was actually proficient in a number of styles, including horror stories for ACG and early Marvel Comics, crime stories for *Premier*, and war illustration for *Soldier of Fortune* magazine. In 1959 he began work at DC (then National Periodical Publications), becoming the primary artist on SUPERMAN'S GIRLFRIEND, LOIS LANE and illustrating dozens of Superman-related stories. He became so identified with Lois Lane (and Lana Lang), that he would often be called upon to redraw their heads on other artists' stories of the period. Schaffenberger had a long run on the Supergirl feature and also worked on WONDER WOMAN and WORLD'S FINEST COMICS before returning to Captain Marvel and the Marvel family when DC revived the characters in 1973.

One of the industry's most acclaimed and prolific artists, **AL WILLIAMSON** began his comics career in 1948 assisting Burne Hogarth on the Sunday *Tarzan* newspaper strip. After honing his skills at publishers like Eastern, ACG, Avon and Toby Press, Williamson became one of the youngest regular artists for E.C.'s classic line of horror and science fiction titles in the mid-1950s. Since then he has worked for nearly every major comic book publisher in America, including DC, Marvel, Dell, Harvey, Fawcett, Charlton, Warren, Western and Dark Horse. He is also a veteran of the syndicated comic strip world, providing art for such classic features as *Rip Kirby, Flash Gordon* and *Star Wars* and enjoying lengthy runs on *Big Ben Bolt* and *Secret Agent Corrigan*. Williamson has won two Eisner Awards and an astonishing five Harvey Awards for Best Inker, and he was named Best Comic Book Artist (Story) by the National Cartoonists Society in 1966.

Heavily influenced by artists Lou Fine and Will Eisner, **MURPHY ANDERSON** entered the comics arena in 1944 as an artist for Fiction House. He took over the *Buck Rogers* comic strip for three years beginning in 1947, and in 1950 he began his lifelong association with DC Comics, pulling double duty as both a full illustrator (the Atomic Knights, Hawkman) and as an inker over other artists' pencil work (Adam Strange, Batman, Superman). Later in his career, Anderson ran Murphy Anderson Visual Concepts, a publishers' support service company. He now enjoys a well-deserved retirement.